To
Con,

I am very glad that your found the family. This book will fill in the history you missed—

Together we will make sure our next chapters will be even better!

Enjoy

Seth

The Power of Positive Destruction

The Power of Positive Destruction

HOW TO TURN A BUSINESS IDEA INTO A REVOLUTION

Seth Merrin

with Carlye Adler

WILEY

Cover art: Mathew Patalano
Cover design: Broken glass © Max Bukovski/Shutterstock; Broken glass © Love the
wind/Shutterstock

Published by John Wiley & Sons, Inc., Hoboken, New Jersey.
Published simultaneously in Canada.

For general information on our other products and services or for technical support, please
contact our Customer Care Department within the United States at (800) 762–2974, outside
the United States at (317) 572–3993 or fax (317) 572–4002.

Wiley publishes in a variety of print and electronic formats and by print-on-demand. Some
material included with standard print versions of this book may not be included in e-books
or in print-on-demand. If this book refers to media such as a CD or DVD that is not included
in the version you purchased, you may download this material at http://booksupport.wiley
.com. For more information about Wiley products, visit www.wiley.com.

Library of Congress Cataloging-in-Publication Data:

ISBN 978–1–119–19642–6 (Hardcover)
ISBN 978–1–119–19643–3 (ePDF)
ISBN 978–1–119–19644–0 (ePub)

Printed in the United States of America

10 9 8 7 6 5 4 3 2 1

I dedicate this book to Anne Heyman, my wife and my soulmate. The girl I fell in love with at 18 and whom I remain madly in love with and miss every minute of every day. To the miracle Anne created and all our remarkable kids from the Agahozo-Shalom Youth Village who make me proud every day and who are shining examples of all that is possible if you give kids a home, a family, love and an opportunity to learn.

To Anne's family, now my family, for sharing Anne with me and with whom I share all the wonderful things that are Anne. To my most incredible family, my mom and dad, my brothers Sam and Jeremy, my sister Esther, my nieces and nephews Maya, Ariel, Ben, Jacob, Isabel, Charlotte, Noah, and Nathan, my brother-in-law Moishik, and sisters-in-law Linda and Holly, and to my unbelievable kids Jason, Jenna, and Jonathan, all of whom helped me get through my darkest hours, who held me together and made me stronger, and for whom I aspire to be the best I can be.

Contents

Acknowledgments

This book would never have been written without the idea and encouragement of Melissa Kanter and the skill of Carlye Adler prying loose my story of the very many mistakes I made, the things I learned, and the strategies I developed from my start-up experiences. The lessons I've learned have mostly come from the people I've worked with past and present, so I would like to thank everyone who has worked at the four companies for all the experiences and lessons that I have learned and shared in this book. Thank you to my sister-in-law, Linda Blum, for all of her help editing the book, and to Cheryl Knopp for always keeping me out of trouble (in and out of this book). Thank you to my agent, Stacey Glick, and to Tula Weis and Julie Kerr and all the folks at Wiley for believing that there was a book inside me and for making this book better. Thank you to my incredible marketing staff for all their input, cover design, and launch strategy. I would like to thank my awesome assistants, Kelly Kiely and Chana Spielberg, for every day they enable me to do my job, and a special call-out to Chana, who in addition to her day job, took on the challenge of making sure this book was written on schedule. I want to thank everyone at Liquidnet for being the change agents who have done all the hard work to make the global financial industry more efficient for investors all over the world. We are only just beginning....

About the Authors

Seth Merrin is an entrepreneur, global business leader, and philanthropist who has reinvented how Wall Street can work for good and use technology to make the markets safer and more efficient for investors.

As founder and CEO of Liquidnet, he has built a different kind of financial services company that has created a global market for institutional asset managers to more efficiently trade stocks and bonds. Liquidnet, named the Number One Broker in the World by Abel/Noser, connects more than 800 of the world's leading asset managers to large-scale equity trading opportunities in 44 markets across five continents. Through Liquidnet for Good and its signature project with the Agahozo-Shalom Youth Village (ASYV) in Rwanda, the company is defining a new vision for how progressive companies can save and improve lives around the world.

Merrin has been named "Innovator of the Decade" by *Advanced Trading* magazine two decades in a row, one of the "100 Most Influential People in Finance" by *Treasury & Risk* magazine, and one of the "Tech 50 for five years in a row by *Institutional Investor.* His innovations have been profiled in more than 50 articles, including *Forbes, Barron's,* and *Crain's New York Business.* Before forming Liquidnet, Merrin cofounded VIE Systems Inc. and Merrin Financial, where he introduced the industry's first order management system, technologies that are now standard on virtually every trading desk around the world. Prior to 1985, Merrin was a Risk Arbitrage Trader for CIBC Oppenheimer. He graduated from Tufts University in 1982 with a degree in Political Science.

● ● ●

Carlye Adler is a best-selling author, book collaborator, and award-winning journalist. Her latest book collaborations include two *New*

York Times best sellers: *The Promise of a Pencil* by Adam Braun, and *The Hard Thing About Hard Things* by Ben Horowitz. She is the coauthor of the *New York Times* best seller *Rebooting Work* with Maynard Webb, and the national best sellers *Behind the Cloud* and *The Business of Changing the World* with Salesforce CEO Marc Benioff. She co-wrote *Startupland* with Mikkel Svane and *The Dragonfly Effect* with Jennifer Aaker and Andy Smith. Her books have been translated into Chinese, German, Greek, Hebrew, Korean, Indonesian, Japanese, Romanian, Russian, Turkish, and Vietnamese.

As a journalist, her writing has been published in *BusinessWeek, FastCompany, Fortune, Forbes, Newsweek, TIME,* and *Wired,* and has been anthologized in *The Best Business Stories of the Year.*

For more information, please visit www.carlyeadler.com.

Introduction: Problems and Opportunities Are Two Sides of a Coin

I'm often told, "You don't have to break *everything*, Seth."

I think you do. All businesses and industries could probably benefit from being broken down and put back together better. In some cases, it's continuous improvement; in others, it is wholesale disruption or positive destruction.

My work life began in the early 1980s when I worked as an intern on Wall Street. Wall Street seemed to me like the center of the universe. The whole world revolved around it. It was fast paced and exciting. It was either where all the smartest people were or where all the smartest people wanted to be. But only a few weeks into the internship, it became clear to me that it was a bit like the Land of Oz. The outside was a picture of well-structured sophistication and complexity. On the inside it was more like the man behind the curtain. I wasn't sure if I was the only one who knew the reality or if I was the only one who wanted to change it.

Either way, seeing past the curtain was the start of my entrepreneurial career, which began at age 24 with my first business, Merrin Financial, a software company that created the first order management system, which automated much of the clerical trading process and ushered in electronic trading. The order management system has since been adopted and is used at every asset management firm around the world. The second company I started was a middleware software company based in New Jersey; the third was a health care technology firm in Silicon Valley; and the fourth is Liquidnet, a global, institutional, electronic brokerage firm, and by far my largest and best company. It's not that I'm a serial entrepreneur as much as I've learned enough from my previous experiences to finally get it right with Liquidnet.

In the pages that follow, I'll tell you my personal story and through it offer real, actionable advice that will resonate with anyone who aspires to be a catalyst of change. You will learn to see the inefficiencies and everyday problems that others dismiss as the cost of doing business, and how to create "unfair competitive advantages" to stack the deck—and win. You'll see how problems in current business models are really opportunities of which to take advantage and learn what you need to know and do to seize those opportunities—no matter where you work. I'll break down my process step-by-step to show you how to successfully start a company and transform an industry.

My voracious appetite for business books has resulted in a lot of knowledge about how others built their businesses and achieved their successes. But most of what I have learned has come from my many mistakes and successes in the four businesses I've started over the years. I believe if you're not making mistakes, you're not trying hard enough. I'll show you what I learned from my missteps: how to build a different kind of company—one that has no titles, no assholes, and not only makes money but gives some of that money back to make the world a better place.

I'll show you how I created several disruptive businesses and reveal how you can, too. With *The Power of Positive Destruction*, you will:

- Discover how to identify problems and turn them into opportunities.
- Understand how to stack the deck in your favor to achieve the best possible chances of success.
- Learn how to build and run a company and design a culture for constant change.
- Acquire new and critical skills to create strategy, sell your disruptive product or service, and negotiate effectively.

Positive destruction can disrupt or transform any company and any industry. It's happening faster and more broadly now than ever before, creating an unlimited number of opportunities for any entrepreneur. But winning in this new world is not easy. The incumbents fight mightily against it and even those who will benefit from change may first express fear. I know firsthand that having a business plan does not mean things go according to plan. I'll give you the real, unpolished version of the struggles we went through, the fights with incumbents, with board members, with investors. I'll reveal the techniques employed, from identifying the opportunities to designing and executing the strategy that you'll need to succeed.

Maybe you're an investor who follows the market and are intrigued by the drama of it and want an inside perspective. Maybe you have no interest working in the financial industry but you believe another industry is ripe for disruption and are interested in strategies and processes that work. Maybe you want to start a business and you know it's no longer good enough to build a company to last but want to build a company of constant change.

In any case, I believe there's something for you in this book, and I hope it inspires you to think differently and tap into your inner change agent to transform your company, your industry, and the world.

PART 1

THE IDEA

1

Any Industry Can Be Disrupted—Positively

One of the most important lessons I've learned in business and in life is that the next great transformational idea can come from the least likely of places—and often when you aren't looking for it. And a technology or a technique, when taken from one industry and applied to another, can be very transformational.

I first learned this from my father, Edward Merrin, a great businessman and extraordinary salesman, albeit an accidental one. By nature my father was more of an artist. That was his passion. When I think about my childhood growing up on the Upper West Side of Manhattan, I remember my father always working on his paintings. He did a bit of everything—still lifes, abstracts, and the naked ladies he went to see pose at the Art Students League of New York. On weekends, he went downtown to Greenwich Village with his paintings in tow and tried to sell them. It didn't go well. Let's just say that Dad owns the biggest collection of Ed Merrin paintings in the world.

Dad's real job was in the family business. My grandfather started a jewelry store, Merrin Jewelers, which was in midtown Manhattan, right across the street from Tiffany & Co. Our family business sold more affordable necklaces, bracelets, and rings than the legendary store with the baby blue boxes. Business wasn't exactly booming. My father worked at Merrin Jewelers from the time he graduated college, but he had little interest in business or in jewelry, and he and his father never got along. It was not exactly a recipe for success.

Luckily, Dad found a way to channel his creativity and find his talents while working in that business. He directed his artistic skills to designing high-end jewelry. It didn't always entice customers. To this day he maintains, "The better the design, the more poorly it sold." He still talks about his favorite piece, a marquee pin with a loop of negative space. No one bought it, and he eventually sold it to his cousin Iris, who purchased it on the condition that he filled the empty space with diamonds. Dad recognized what was important and agreed to the request. "Money is money," he said. "Even if it destroyed the whole design." The tangential lesson learned: Give the customer what she thinks she wants.

At the same time, Dad was always innovative, always giving the customer what he did not *yet* know he wanted. Such was the case with the 14k gold toothpick "for the man who had every-thing." It retailed for $7.50. His first buyer was Joseph Welch, the head counsel for the U.S. Army while it was under investigation by Joseph McCarthy for Communist activities. Sales ballooned from there. Merrin Jewelers sold 10,000 gold toothpicks, and to this day people still carry them around (or sell them on eBay for $149.99).

Still, Dad didn't think those numbers were good enough. "We should have sold hundreds of thousands of them!" And shortly after, he did figure out a way to move more merchandise than he ever had before. Dad started advertising. He took out a small ad in the *Wall Street Journal* and then double-page ads in *Diners Club* magazine. These were not chic ads; they were utilitarian, show-ing the objects and their prices. They worked. Orders started to come in. He then created an entire catalog. At the time, jewelry wasn't advertised like this and mail order hadn't been done in this industry. Dad's idea stemmed from seeing the ads for knit-ted caps from Maine in the margins of *The New Yorker* magazine and the Sears and L.L. Bean catalogs that showed up in the mail-room. But Dad believed it was applicable in his business too, and mail order for jewelry worked—it soon became 70 percent of the business.

While Merrin Jewelers expanded its business with mail order in a way it never could have had it relied on in-store sales alone, Dad was a consummate salesman as soon as he got in front of the customer. "You'd be stupid not to buy this," he'd say, and some-how instead of seeming pushy or cocky, he'd pull it off. He always closed the deal.

The Next Great Idea Comes from Anywhere

Dad taught me to borrow from other industries and that selling is all about relationships, but those weren't the only lessons. He showed me that the next great business idea comes from anywhere—and it's often right in front of you. You just have to be ready to see it.

My parents married in 1957 and honeymooned in Acapulco. It was a great trip not only because it was the start of their new life as a couple, but it kick-started a new stage in my father's artistic pursuits. While in Mexico, Dad fell in love with pre-Columbian art. He visited some dealers while there and purchased three pieces: two bowls and a terra-cotta figure—all for $69. He used one of the bowls in a window display, draping pieces of jewelry over it. It did attract interest, but not for the jewelry: Someone came in and asked, "How much for the bowl?" Dad sold it to him for $35, and with this sale he started a whole new career as an art dealer.

Interestingly, Dad had no background in this type of art. He was first-generation American and not the most inspired student in school. But now, he found something that fascinated him. He developed a passion for pre-Columbian cultures and art and started educating himself. He read every book on the subject. He went back to Mexico and bought more pre-Columbian art and began selling it out of our family's apartment.

This led to his own business idea—and his lifelong work and passion. When he was 40, with four children to support, he opened his own business, the Merrin Gallery, which operated in office space upstairs from the jewelry store. My grandfather was steadfastly against the idea, but my mother was always supportive. He spent their life savings—$4,000—on building the business. It was a financial drain: the phone bill was often paid three months late and we ate a lot of pasta.

WHEN TO START A BUSINESS?

Great start-up lore leads us to believe that all great businesses were started by a 20-something in a college dorm room. TechCrunch founder Michael Arrington even wrote a blog post called "Internet Entrepreneurs Are Like Professional Athletes, They Peak Around 25."

But the reality is that founders over 25 are not over the hill. In fact, according to a study by Bloomberg Beta, the most ideal start-up candidates are more likely to be in their late 30s, and 38 percent of founders were over 40.[1] Another study, funded by the Kauffman Foundation, revealed that the typical successful founder was 40 years old, and there are twice as many successful entrepreneurs over 50 than there are successful founders under 25.[2]

As my dad discovered, being 40 does not make it too late to start a business. Donald Fisher was 40 and had no experience in retail when he and his wife, Doris, opened the first Gap store in San Francisco. Ray Kroc, who built the world's biggest franchise, didn't buy his first McDonald's until he was 52. Vera Wang was a figure skater and journalist before entering the fashion industry at 40. And Sam Walton founded the first Walmart when he was 44.[3]

Of course, there are many people who started companies before the age of 25 who have done tremendously well. But for all the hype, success at such a young age is just much harder to achieve. I started my first business at 24. I didn't know what I was lacking, but it was a lot. I didn't have any reputation, connections, business experience, credibility, or track record. All of that limits your opportunity. By the time I started Liquidnet, my fourth business, I had all of these things and knew their value.

Dad did well in his new endeavor. He knew how to bring in business, and he kept incorporating creative ideas to attract customers. There was no storefront to his second-floor gallery so he set up beautiful displays in a four-foot window on 54th Street and people were captivated enough to get in the creaky old elevator and come to his gallery to see what he was selling. He found a mentor at the Museum of Natural History who helped extend his knowledge. With increased understanding he expanded into all forms of ancient art—Ancient Greek, Roman, Egyptian.

With Dad's keen eye for what was beautiful and his consummate selling skills—"You need this for your collection!" he often said—the gallery, over time, became one of the top ancient art galleries in the world. *What I learned: pursue your passion with self-confidence, education, and the goal of being the best in the world at it.*

Today, we'd call my father's change in career course a "pivot," and while it was a risk to bet the farm on his passion for ancient art, my father, like any entrepreneur, was no gambler. He pursued his passion fully knowing it would work out, and he didn't rely on luck to make that happen. He did everything he could to stack the deck in his favor.

With all businesses there are many variables that are outside of our control: markets go up and down and trends come and go. We need to control what we can as much as we possibly can. Lock in your suppliers, control your costs, launch with a critical mass of customers, and, most importantly, *make sure you have an unfair competitive advantage that you can articulate and your prospects will understand within 30 seconds.* My test of how good your unfair competitive advantage is and how well you articulate it is: when trying it out on family and friends, the response should be, "You would have to be an idiot not to buy it or try it."

At the Merrin Gallery my father succeeded by becoming an expert in his field. Specifically, he educated himself on every culture, civilization, and period of ancient art that he sold. He combined that with an incredible eye for buying only the best-quality pieces. By focusing on a rather narrow niche of the art world and through a lot of hard work, Dad became one of the foremost ancient art dealers in the world. His knowledge, his eye, and his insistence on buying the most unique and rare pieces created his unique selling proposition for just about every sale he made and created an unfair competitive advantage for himself.

His customers knew that anything they bought from Dad would add to the value and prestige of their collection. When making a sale, Dad would explain why a piece was the best of its kind in 30 seconds—which was absolutely critical. Then, once his customer was interested, he would delve into much greater detail.

LESSONS FROM DAD ON HOW TO STACK THE DECK

- Borrow from other industries to disrupt your own.
- Pursue your passion with self-confidence, education, and the goal of being the best in the world.
- Perfect your pitch: Make your case within 30 seconds.
- Know how to sell.

Where Can You Find the Edge?

I recently had a conversation with a friend in the engineering industry who was looking for ways to grow his company and thinking about acquisitions. That's justified. You can grow a company organically—by gradually increasing sales—or inorganically—

through acquisitions. Growing through acquisition should be a focus, but it shouldn't be the only focus. It should not take the place of or take precedence over thinking creatively about how to organically grow the business, create competitive advantages, and positively disrupt your industry. *I've learned that the way to really grow your business is to spend time thinking about how to gain an edge by doing something faster, better, and more efficiently than your competitors.* These are transformational opportunities that most organizations simply miss.

For too many, it's all about the 3 Ps of marketing: Product, Price, Promotion. But that's not how great businesses are built or managed in today's environment. *In order to stack the deck, you have to find one or two or three things that the clients are most concerned about or value the most, and solve those.*

What do I mean? A terrific example comes from the cement industry. How do you disrupt the cement industry? Look at what Cemex did. This Mexico-based company saw problems with the traditional way the industry operated. Historically, construction companies bought massive amounts of cement, just to have on site. This tied up an enormous amount of money and required space to store the materials. Moreover, companies never had the exact quantity of cement they needed—they ended up with too much or too little. (Even being off by a small amount translates to a big problem when you consider the size of buildings or complexes). But this is how it was done—until Cemex changed the game.

In the early 1990s, Cemex was on the verge of bankruptcy, and it looked to other organizations—FedEx, Domino's Pizza, and 911 dispatch centers—for insights on how to improve. It ultimately implemented a just-in-time delivery mechanism borrowed from the manufacturing industry. Cemex delivered the exact amount of cement as the project is being developed as it was needed. With that seemingly basic advance, customers no longer had their cash tied up in cement they didn't yet need, and they no longer were storing excess or running out of material. Think about the most important things for your customers. They want just-in-time delivery. They don't want to spend more than they have to, and they don't want any costly delays due to lack of building material. By addressing those two concerns, and by efficiently using technology including satellites and software modeled after the 911 emergency systems, Cemex was able to fulfill orders within a short time.[4] From near-bankruptcy, Cemex became one of the world's largest building materials suppliers and cement producers. In 2003, *Wired* lauded its efficient "just-in-time" delivery system and named Cemex one of the world's top five "masters of innovation, technology, and strategic vision"[5] and in 2008 the company ranked it just behind Google in a survey of companies reshaping the global economy.[6] It is a cement company. Enough said . . . .

Of course, this is similar to what Dell did when it changed the computer industry. IBM, Digital Computer, and other computer companies used to order massive amounts of parts that they would store in inventory. This would cost money, tie up resources, and create lots of overhead. Dell implemented just-in-time delivery, which resulted in driving the price point of its computers way down and its margins way up. Utilizing this approach, Dell achieved positive cash flows as their customers paid them before Dell had to pay their suppliers, giving Dell access to "free cash" to finance their operations and a massive competitive edge.

Southwest Airlines offers another great example of a company disrupting a stodgy industry by thinking differently. Southwest was founded in 1967 and started operations in 1971 as a small airline with three planes. It flew only within the state of Texas. There's not a large disruptive technology component to Southwest's story but rather a hard look at solving a key problem for a large segment of customers, delivering the cheapest flights possible. To solve for this, Southwest looked to where serious cost savings and efficiencies could be implemented, and where services could be improved to increase customer satisfaction. It established four major points of differentiation that gave it an edge.

1. Only fly one type of plane. Southwest decided early on to only fly and support one plane type: the Boeing 737. This saved a tremendous amount of money on maintenance costs, personnel training, spare parts inventories, compatible equipment to load and equip the planes, and more.
2. Use point-to-point flying as opposed to the traditional hub-and-spoke network. This approach avoided the costly plane delays of waiting and coordinating connecting flights, improved margins by having more flight time per plane, and boosted customer satisfaction by reducing flight delays and flying passengers directly.

3. Avoid frills; just offer cheap, simple service. At the time when every passenger enjoyed full meals and snacks, Southwest positioned itself as the "no-frills" airline. It did away with assigned seats and meals. It focused on unloading, cleaning, and restocking the plane and boarding the next set of passengers in 20 minutes as opposed to the roughly 90 minutes it took the competition. This enabled the airline to get an additional flight per day out of each aircraft—vastly increasing its margins.
4. Focus on a fun-loving culture. Southwest realized early on that treating their employees better results in a better customer experience.

Until 2008, when the founder, Herb Kelleher, stepped down from running Southwest, the airline had the best on-time performance record of any domestic carrier and its market capitalization was almost twice that of all six of their domestic competitors combined.[7] Unfortunately, the airline has stumbled and has lost both of those positions since Kelleher retired.

What's Israel and Irrigation Got to Do with It?

I learned many lessons on how to build a disruptive business, but in the beginning, when I was first thinking about my career, I had no idea what I wanted to do. My older brother, Jeremy, went to work with my grandfather in the jewelry store. My younger brother, Sam, who inherited Dad's passion for art, went to work with Dad in the gallery. I was the middle son, different from my two brothers, and had no passion, inclination, or desire to do anything related to jewelry or art.

I wasn't the most motivated student, but I was passionate about my extracurricular pursuits. When I was in junior high school I became involved in Young Judaea, a Jewish, Zionist, youth group. Young Judaea was a transformational experience for me. This was a peer-led movement and there were role models who were cool—they were smart and worldly and I was motivated to be like them. We just hung out and talked, and at first it was something to do on a Sunday night. We went to regional conventions a few times a year, and when I noticed there were cute girls who also attended, I ramped up my involvement. I grew up in a kosher home, one that adhered to Jewish customs and instilled a sense of Jewish identity, promoting charity and giving back. I had my *bar mitzvah* in Israel, and my parents even thought of emigrating to Israel. Yet it was during my time in Young Judaea that I started to believe in a higher purpose and gain a greater sense of Jewish identity and a connection to Israel. I started to care about things that I found unjust, like the persecution of the Soviet Jews, and I had a feeling that together we could change things—that we could make a difference. Arik Einstein's folk song "You and I" captured the spirit of Young Judea and served as our anthem: "You and I will change the world." I was introduced to the idea of *Tikkun olam,* or "repairing the world," *and that we had a responsibility to make the world a better place.* My commitment to the program grew and ultimately I served as president of the metropolitan New York area.

The Young Judaea program culminated in "Year Course," a gap year between high school and college, with much of it spent on a kibbutz, a communal farm, in Israel.

So, at 18, when my high school friends were starting college, I went to work on a four-year old kibbutz in Israel's southern desert— in the middle of nowhere. My job involved driving a tractor, picking Galia melons (a hybrid melon that looks like cantaloupe on the outside and honeydew on the inside, which is much sweeter than either one), and packing fruit. We woke at 3 A.M. to go down to the fields to pick these melons and brought teaspoons to scoop and eat melon as we worked. We started the day in winter coats, and by 5 A.M. we were dripping in sweat. I learned about cultivating crops (we grew peppers and onions as well), pest control, and fertilizer and irrigation.

I loved it. It wasn't just about hanging out with new friends, getting dirty, and the satisfaction that came with hard work. It was something else: we helped make the desert bloom. We planted in sand dunes and created something different and beautiful and lasting. This was so clear to me as I rode the bus from Jerusalem through the Judean Hills, to the Arava Desert, and then all of a sudden there were green patches, a result of the hard work done on the kibbutzes. We were pioneers—working the land and building the future. It was easy to become passionate about it when we saw such progress.

Who thinks about having a farm in the middle of the desert? That fascinates me. And how Israel did it fascinates me more. Israel created farms in the desert where water was the scarcest of resources.

How do you possibly make growing vegetables efficient and cost effective in the middle of the desert—a place where you have no natural resources: no water, no soil, and no fertilizer? The answer is you figure out how to solve for it in a new way. The most advanced farming and irrigation system in the world was created out of necessity. Up until this time irrigation happened naturally, with rain, by digging trenches, or with sprinklers. Think about what a waste it would be to use sprinklers spraying water, which is so precious in the desert, at places where there were no plants. Instead, something called drip irrigation was invented on a kibbutz so that every drip of water was targeted to have a nurturing effect on a plant. It sounds complicated, but it's so simple—just a plastic pipe with holes drilled in it where the plants are. On professional farms, you plant in evenly measured spaces—two or four inches apart, depending on the plant—so this is quite easy to target. Every drop of water is used by the plant; not one is wasted. It's so smart, and so simple. As my father would say, "You'd be stupid not to do it."

POSITIVE DESTRUCTION 101

If you are not thinking about how you are going to do things differently and the competition *is* thinking about their offering that way, you're putting yourself in a very vulnerable position.

You need to employ every transformational strategy in your arsenal. This is not something you think about once a year. You think about it constantly. This is the most difficult work—and where the most creativity comes in. Three pieces of advice on how to do it:

- **Dissect your business.** What are the three most important things your customer base would want that they don't currently have? What would improve their business or lives that they are not getting today? What are the things that if you could change and deliver would give you an unfair competitive advantage?

- **Understand this takes time.** I spent months and months thinking about ideas. And I threw out dozens. *Good is not good enough.* But with focused attention, you'll get to great.

- **Live by the 30-second rule.** Your concept has to be presented and the concept understood in 30 seconds or less, and everyone has to immediately see how awesome it would be or that they would be nuts not to have it. Then you'll know you've nailed it.

This type of thinking and the other technological advances it inspired—solenoids, or little sensors that turned the water on and off, technologies that tested the soil and gave you feedback as to its alkalinity—helped Israel become a world leader in agriculture in spite of the fact that it's not naturally conducive to agriculture.

Those are the kind of results that happen when you break ideas down and build new systems from the ground up. That's the kind of positive destruction practice anyone wanting success needs to adopt.

Notes

1. Ian Rose, "Over 40? Data Says You Could Be the Perfect Entrepreneur." BBC, October 24, 2014; www.bbc.com/news/business-29660624
2. Krisztina Z. Holly, "Why Great Entrepreneurs Are Older than You Think." *Forbes,* January 15, 2014; www.forbes.com/sites/krisztinaholly/2014/01/15/why-great-entrepreneurs-are-older-than-you-think/
3. Richard Feloni, "23 People Who Became Highly Successful after Age 40." *Business Insider,* July 15, 2015; time.com/3958885/highly-successful-people-after-age-40/
4. Joel Millman, "Hard Times for Cement Man." *Wall Street Journal,* December 11, 2008; www.wsj.com/articles/SB122894691555195919
5. Nathaniel Parish Flannery, "Cemented in Place: Do Leadership Issues at Mexican Cement Giant Cemex Pose a Risk for Investors?" *Forbes,* April 14, 2011; www.forbes.com/sites/nathanielparishflannery/2011/04/14/cemented-in-place-do-leadership-issues-at-mexican-cement-giant-cemex-pose-a-risk-for-investors/
6. Iris R. Firstenberg and Moshe F. Rubenstein, *Extraordinary Outcomes: Shaping an Otherwise Unpredictable Future* (Hoboken, NJ: John Wiley & Sons, August 25, 2015), 110, 120–122.
7. Joe Brancatelli, "Southwest's Seven Secrets for Success." *Entrepreneur,* July 8, 2008; www.entrepreneur.com/article/195762

CHAPTER 2

Ask WTF

After a year in Israel, I returned to the United States ready to take on college at Tufts University outside Boston. Tufts was an expected part of my trajectory. My dad, uncle, and brother all went to Tufts, and I never contemplated other options. We call it "Merrin University." But once there, I was unsure of what I wanted to do. I majored in political science, a common default major at the time. I didn't prove to be much of a student and didn't earn stellar grades.

I really liked computers, introduced to me by my uncle, who was one of the earliest and largest Apple dealers. It was the early 1980s, and I was the only one that I knew in college with a personal computer. It was an Apple IIe, which I used to play Space Invaders, Defenders, and Pac-Man, and occasionally I used its word processing software for a paper. I was mostly concerned with having fun and not really thinking about how my classes could relate to my future. I was excited about one course in my schedule, though—Introduction to Computer Programming; it was offered pass/fail. I enrolled and had to drop it because I was failing. I took an elective course in stocks and bonds. There, I got a solid B. I didn't know where I was heading; I took those courses because they looked interesting, not because I believed they were a stepping-stone to a career. Similarly, the other classes I most remember—Byzantine history, art history, and Yiddish literature—were personal intellectual interests, not potential professional pursuits.

Four years went by incredibly quickly. Before I knew it, I was graduating. I had a plan to move back to New York. But that was the extent of the plan. As far as work, I had no idea what I would do.

In a way, it didn't matter. I didn't expect to stay in New York for too long. My real goal was to spend another year in Israel on the kibbutz with Anne, my girlfriend from my year in Israel. Therefore, I was only looking for a temporary job, something to make a little money—enough to save for the trip. I went up and down Columbus Avenue in Manhattan looking for a job as a waiter. I was rejected by every restaurant—at least twice.

While a college degree was not enough to land a job as a waiter, my father called in a favor with a buddy of his on Wall Street and secured an interview for an internship.

Nate Gantcher was a client of the gallery and a fellow trustee of Tufts University. At the time, he was the vice president of Oppenheimer & Co. (He later was the co-CEO.) I got the interview, not on my merit, but because of my father's connections. But I went to the meeting prepared with knowledge about the company and an interest in the way Wall Street worked.

ENTERING A ROOM IS SO MUCH EASIER THROUGH AN OPEN DOOR

With social networking and a connected world, it's easier than ever to get an introduction to job opportunities, and that is a big first step. But this only opens a door—everything else is up to you. So many people come into our offices today through a warm introduction. But when they ask the basics of what Liquidnet does, I lose interest in a few seconds.

Today, information is ubiquitous and to keep the door open, you should do a tremendous amount of homework before you walk in the door. *You want to be even smarter about the business than the person interviewing you. People hire people who take initiative.* If you do the homework, it won't guarantee you the job, but if you don't do your homework, you have not stacked the deck in your favor—and you've increased the likelihood that you've helped shut that door behind you. Don't let it slam.

When Opportunity Knocks, Take It

I landed the gig at Oppenheimer and soon learned the internship was designed to expose me to many facets of the organization by cycling me through the many divisions at the company. My first job was in the back office of Oppenheimer. There I learned what happened after the trade was made. It involved at least 50 different steps; it was entirely manual; and it involved entering essentially the same information into multiple computer systems, and it was impossible to scale. In the 1960s and 1970s when the New York Stock Exchange (NYSE) was executing around 10 million shares per day, the inefficiencies of Wall Street's back offices led to the closure of the NYSE on Tuesday and Thursday afternoons to give the back offices more time to process the trades. It also led to the demise of a number of brokerage firms—much of it due to errors associated with these manual processes. Not much had changed in the early 1980s. This is how it worked when I started: In order for the trading desk to execute an order on behalf of a client, they handed me a paper ticket. My job was to look up the accounts for whom that trade was executed and manually write a separate ticket for each of those accounts. These tickets then had to be entered into separate accounting and clearing systems. The account information was kept in a loose-leaf binder. It wasn't even alphabetized.

It seemed inefficient—I definitely wondered WTF—and I wanted to change it, not because I was looking for any accolades, but just because I wanted it to work more efficiently—I wanted it to work in a way that made sense. I introduced alphabetizing the accounts by cutting and pasting the accounts back into the loose-leaf notebooks.

Believe it or not, this was seen as a big innovation since no one else had thought of it! But, of course, this small change, while helpful, hardly solved the overall problem, which was that capturing and organizing information manually was a ridiculous process that couldn't scale. Not having the records automated in any way meant that it took hours to enter information into multiple accounting and clearing systems. It was mind-numbing, error-prone work. I hated it.

I thought the binder was archaic, but it was 1982 and this is how things were done. No one had experience with computers. The PC was still seen as a toy.

I went to see Nate and informed him of this backward process and time suck. Only years later did I realize what a privilege it was to have direct access to Nate. In a way, I was like a kid in a candy store, excited about everything around me and eager to share my thoughts with anyone who would listen. I think Nate liked my passion and appreciated the viewpoints. At the time I had no appreciation for how busy he was.

ALWAYS HAVE AN OPEN DOOR POLICY

Today, inspired by Nate, who always welcomed my thoughts even when I was an intern, I've instituted an open door policy. I encourage everyone to come into my office and share their viewpoints. I give everybody a fair hearing, regardless of how long they've been at the organization or how senior they are. In fact, I particularly welcome newcomers and want to hear their ideas. I routinely sit down with people when they start and ask them to come back to me after a month or two and report on the good and the bad they've experienced to that point.

I also went to the head of the back office, complaining about how inefficient their process was and how a computer could solve this easily. There would be so many other benefits: you could calculate real-time positions, eliminate clerical time, provide more accurate information, eradicate multiple data entries, reduce errors, save money, and scale as volumes increased.

The people in the back office were very experienced in back-office operations, but they didn't know much about computers. Therefore, they didn't understand how computers could improve their processes. I even approached the head of the technology group with my ideas, but that didn't go very far, either. At the time, mainframes or mini-computers were used to run back-office systems, and they were very expensive to program and create new functionality for, making them impractical. Additionally, there was a big disconnect between the business and technology units. At the time, business people didn't understand technology, and technology people didn't understand the business. That's changed over the past 30 years as now everyone understands and appreciates (or at least takes for granted) the role tech plays in running and enhancing the business. But that was not the case back then.

In fact, at the time, the processes in place were simply how business was conducted. No one viewed inefficiency as a problem that needed to be solved. Wall Street was making so much money, the idea of using computers to make things more efficient and to save money was never really considered. The solution to the disorganized hassle was just to hire more back-office staff and have them take care of it.

In fairness to those managers, there was no need to change a system they believed was working. *I learned that there are too few people who can see outside of what they know beyond how it is to how it could be.* There was another complicating factor, too—entering data into a computer was seen as clerical work. It was not seen as "trading." The paper tickets and the handwritten notes were considered the "art" of trading. As a newcomer with a different perspective, I saw little art in the process, only that it could benefit from a little more science.

It wasn't long before my rotation in the back office was over and I was moved to the floor of the American Stock Exchange. On my first day, I was introduced to a guy who was assigned to train me. He went to lunch at noon—and he never came back. I didn't know what happened, but I knew I was in the right place at the right time. I got his job. Not a bad first day of work.

Again, I had no idea what I was doing. I found it fascinating, exciting, and frustrating to see how Wall Street worked. In this particular job, my role was to pass orders received from Oppenheimer's brokers to the floor traders to get them executed. An order got called to a clerk upstairs, and then it was sent to me. I figured out where the trade was supposed to go, gave it to the floor trader to execute, and I then relayed it back to the trading desk. If it sounds backwards, inefficient, and nonsensical, that's because it was. It was also easy. No one would need more than an hour of training to do the job well.

I found the whole thing maddening. I was only an intern and probably had no business doing this, but every day after trading hours were over I went upstairs to Nate's office and told him about everything that was wrong with this system and how I thought we could fix it.

IF IT AIN'T BROKE, FIX IT

Business and technology are dynamic and people who can see beyond business as usual—people who can see and envision new and more efficient ways of doing that business—will create competitive advantages for themselves, their customers, and their businesses.

I was quick to speak up, but I knew that if I raised a problem, I should propose a solution. Otherwise, I was just complaining. After some time there, I realized things could be changed for the better after spending time listening, absorbing, and understanding how technology could help improve the efficiency of the back office. I wasn't afraid to bring these thoughts to someone who could help implement change.

If you see things that can be improved, come with solutions—and you can achieve an enormous impact. At Liquidnet, the company I run today, I often say, "I want everyone at this company to feel that they *should* speak up." *It's so much better to have hundreds of minds taking responsibility for improving the company rather than just a few in management.*

If You Find the Problem, Find the Solution

Wall Street was hardly the only industry ripe for innovation. Many established industries had been at this precipice before—and found success in transforming their established ways. And though it can take time—sometimes decades—new ways are ultimately validated. One of the best examples comes from the story of W. Edwards

Deming, an obscure American engineer, statistician, and NYU professor who became a preeminent expert on business management and process improvement.

Today, Deming is recognized as the father of the Total Quality Management (TQM) movement, a strategy for continuously improving performance at every level, and in all areas of responsibility. Back when he was first espousing these theories, the United States had emerged as the global industrial power after World War II and no one in the United States took him very seriously. But in Japan they did. Japanese industrial leaders were intrigued by research he did during World War II and in 1947 invited him to deliver a series of lectures on his quality-control principles. They knew that in order to succeed, they needed to sell products to the world.[1] But at the time, quality was an issue, as Japan's products—from TVs to radios to cars—were known for their shoddiness. In fact, "Made in Japan" had such a negative connotation that some companies set up plants in the Japanese village of Usa, which allowed them to say their products were "Made in USA."[2] True story.

Deming was tapped in the summer of 1950 to lead seminars where he trained hundreds of engineers, managers, and scholars. He spoke to top management, including the cofounder of Sony.[3] His message: improving quality would reduce expenses while increasing productivity and market share.[4] He rebuked management procedures like production quotas, performance ratings, and individual bonuses, calling them "inherently unfair" and "detrimental to quality." He said customers would get better products and services when workers were encouraged to use their minds as well as their hands on the job.[5]

One of Deming's principles was "Put everybody in the company to work to accomplish the transformation. The transformation is everybody's job."[6] That meant that any worker could pull the emergency stop when they saw a defect in the product or process or generally when something went wrong. Not only did they have the authority to do so, *but they were expected to do so.*

A number of Japanese manufacturers, including Panasonic, Sony, and Honda, applied these techniques and experienced previously unknown levels of quality and productivity. The improved quality combined with the lowered cost created new international demand for Japanese products, ushering in the "Japanese postwar economic miracle." Japan became the second most powerful economy in the world in less than a decade.[7]

Deming didn't receive renown in the United States until 30 years later when he was featured in a 1980 NBC TV documentary about the increasing industrial competition from Japan. Japanese products were taking market share. Sony and Panasonic TVs and stereos replaced Zenith and General Electric. Toyotas, Datsuns (now Nissan), and Hondas became more hip with younger people than GM, Ford, and Chrysler brands. Ford became one of the first large American corporations to look to Deming for help. Ford was hemorrhaging hundreds of millions of dollars per year in the late 1970s and early 1980s and losing market share. One of the first things Deming told them was that 85 percent of quality problems with the cars was the result of management errors.[8] The executives were surprised, and egos were a bit beaten up when Deming asked them, "Do you have a constancy of purpose?"[9] Deming explained that it was up to management to correct system problems and foster an environment that allowed workers to reach their potential. It was management's job to incent workers to take responsibility in solving issues, quell fears workers had around identifying quality problems, and eradicate practices like numerical quotas, which he said were counterproductive.[10]

While Ford found itself struggling in the late '1970s, it had once been wildly disruptive. Henry Ford adopted the assembly line process to manufacture cars, which reduced the time it took to build a car from 12 hours to around 2½ and created an unfair competitive advantage in both cost and scalability. With that he was able to drive the growth of Ford Motor Company from 10,000 cars manufactured in 1908 to 472,350 cars in 1915 to 933,720 cars in 1920.[11]

But as Ford kept cutting cost and price, it also stopped innovating. In the 1920s, GM, driven by consumer research, came out with a "car for every purse and purpose," while Ford was still pumping out the same old things. When asked about available colors, Henry Ford famously said, "any color … as long as it's black." That unwillingness to change didn't play well. In 1921, Ford sold about 66 percent of all the cars built in the United States; by 1926, only five years later, this share fell to approximately 33 percent; and in 1927, it fell to about 15 percent.[12] GM overtook Ford, and eventually the Japanese manufacturers did, too.

How did Ford turn things around? Deming. In 1986, Ford came out with the profitable Taurus-Sable line of cars, which the Ford chairman wrote "had their roots directly in Deming's teachings."[13] That year, for the first time since the 1920s, Ford's earnings exceeded those of GM, and Ford became the most profitable American auto company.

Companies that go about business as usual and don't look for better ways of doing things, that don't continue to innovate, are bound to decline. But with the right energies invested in change, things can be turned around. Ford's story can give hope to any company in any industry.

After all, there are many other examples. In 1997, Steve Jobs took back the reins from Gil Amelio, who was running Apple Computer. The company had lost its edge and was running out of money. It was 90 days from going bankrupt. Apple's market capitalization was $3 billion. When Michael Dell was asked what could be done to fix the company, he responded, "What would I do? I'd shut it down and give the money back to the shareholders."[14]

But we all know that's not how Apple's story ended, not even close. Instead of being sold for scrap, it started innovating again and soon entered into consumer electronics, which now accounts for the vast majority of the company's revenue. Apple, which, since the launch of the iPhone in 2008, has been one of the most valuable companies by market cap,[15] shows us you can innovate in any industry, at any inflection point in a company. It all comes down to determining the big idea—and continuously coming up with new big ideas because things are ever changing. Or as Steve Jobs wrote in a company memo in 2006: "Based on today's stock market close, Apple is worth more than Dell. Stocks go up and down and things may be different tomorrow, but I thought it was worth a moment of reflection today."[16]

In another example, in the mid-1990s Marvel, the iconic comic book publisher, filed for bankruptcy. In an effort to turn the company around, Marvel decided to try leveraging their brands into movies. They sold licenses to other studios and they saw the X-Men and Spider-Man movies make fortunes for others. But the movies weren't great, and Marvel thought it could do better. The concept had been tested—moviegoers were attracted to the titles. What would happen if Marvel were in charge and produced the movies themselves?

The company hired directors who were huge comic book fans, and unlike the licensed versions of the films, these adaptations didn't take comic books as literally. They added twists and humor to the stories that were not in the series themselves. Marvel took more risks and applied more creativity in transferring comics from pages to screen. In 2008, Marvel released the first Iron Man movie. Although Iron Man was a much more obscure superhero, the movie was incredibly successful because of Marvel's different approach. Seven years later, in 2015, the Marvel franchise had produced 12 films, grossing over $8.9 billion in the box office, and ranks as the highest-grossing film franchise in both the United States and worldwide, according to boxofficemojo.com.

Business Is Just a Set of Problems to Solve

In my early days at Oppenheimer, no one was receptive to the ideas I had—not the managers or even the computer department. But in my final rotation, through the risk arbitrage hedge fund, I found an interested audience. This rotation offered a very different environment than I had previously experienced. There weren't that many hedge funds at the time, and Oppenheimer therefore had the pick of the best and brightest individuals to do this very sophisticated work. This wasn't just about trading but about investing based on assessing probability of a merger or acquisition being completed. The incentive compensation for hedge funds has a lot to do with the receptivity to new ideas. If you can increase your returns and/or decrease expenses, it will have a direct impact on your compensation.

I found working in this division and working with these very bright people inspiring. I read everything I could find on the subject and worked long hours. I discovered something I was passionate about, and my life became very focused on work. I was still just an intern, but I was the first one at the office in the morning and the last one out at night. I was like a sponge trying to absorb knowledge from everyone and everything around me. When the head of the hedge fund cleared out his bookshelves, I took every book he wanted to toss. I read with great interest dense materials on the markets, risk arbitrage, how to read financial statements, and, of course, *Security Analysis* by Benjamin Graham and David Dodd—Warren Buffett's bible.

While the people in the department were very smart, and I learned an incredible amount from them, the way the system worked, even in this special section, was still epically inefficient. We managed money on behalf of several accounts and everything was tracked on paper, in pencil. At the end of each day, I took all of the tickets and adjusted the positions in the portfolio by hand: if we bought a stock,

I erased the amount and added it to our position; if we sold, I erased the amount and deducted it. Then, I went to the copy machine and printed out copies to distribute to everyone. We went through a lot of pencils, erasers, and paper. More importantly, risk arbitrage is very formula driven. It's all about calculating the spreads between the deal price and the price of the stock being acquired, factoring probability of close and time for an expected internal rate of return. This was a perfect job for a computer, but calculating the spreads—the very core of the investment strategy—was done by hand.

There was only one computer in the firm, a Tandy RadioShack, which was kept in a back corner of the office. I knew that it would be fairly easy for the computer to calculate our positions in real time, and I also knew that if we could calculate the spreads faster than our competition, we could buy and sell stock faster and cheaper than they could, giving us an unfair competitive advantage, and boost our returns. I went to that one computer and taught myself Multiplan, an early spreadsheet program, which was developed by Microsoft. I used the program to generate real-time position reports, and I pitched the idea of using the computer to run analytics in real time. The head of the unit agreed immediately.

It worked. As the price of stocks changed during the day, spreads between the stocks made some trades profitable and others not. Tracking the spreads on a computer gave us many more opportunities to execute profitable trades than our competitors, who were still calculating the spreads manually. This gave us an unfair competitive advantage to produce greater returns for our funds.

HOW TO COME UP WITH THE NEXT BIG IDEA

The venture capital industry has grown into an enormous source of start-up financing, funding close to $50 billion in start-ups in 2014, according to data from the National Venture Capital Association and PricewaterhouseCoopers.[17] It has never been easier, cheaper, or faster to create disruptive companies using technology and someone else's money. All you need is the right idea and the principles in this book.

If you haven't had the big epiphany and you're looking for opportunities for a new business or an adjacent business, this is a process that I've used and found helpful for just about any type of investment:

1. **Start with a macro event that is an absolute.** Take a look at the macro environment and investigate what's happening. For instance, as of this

writing: Fact: interest rates are at a historic low. Therefore, it's pretty much a fact—an absolute—that interest rates will only go up from here. Fact: Post financial crisis regulation of Basel III and Dodd-Frank have increased the amount of capital banks must maintain and limits the type of risks banks can take on. Therefore, banks cannot and are not lending to smaller businesses or less creditworthy borrowers. Fact: Oil prices declined by more than 50 percent over a seven-month period from June 2014 to January 2015. With that magnitude of decline there are huge winners and losers. The decline puts around $750 back into the pockets of the average American consumer. Russia loses around $2 billion in revenues for every dollar decline in the price of oil. China is the largest net importer of oil; Japan imports virtually all of its oil; India imports 75 percent of its oil.[18]

2. **Determine what opportunities will arise from the change.** Start thinking about all of the ripple effects that will happen. It can be in your industry, or it can be in any industry. Ask yourself: "Who wins and loses when the price of oil drops so far so fast; when interest rates rise; when capital requirements at banks are tightened?" "What are the opportunities in virtually any area that are going to be affected here?" And then ask yourself, "Where is it that I can add value?"

It was my experience with automating one small piece of the risk arbitrage business that started me thinking about the potential for creating a more sophisticated "order management system" (OMS) and the impact that such a system could have on the industry. I started to believe it could revolutionize the way trading was done. But now, just as I found something I loved, when I was finally having some influence and was seeing progress, the rotation in the risk arbitrage department was over. In fact, the short-term job was coming to a close. It was almost time to leave for Israel. But before I left, the chief financial officer asked to speak with me.

"I thought you would just be a rich brat, but it turns out you have become indispensable," he said. "We'd like to hire you when you get back."

Surprisingly enough, I turned out to be indispensable because of something unexpected—seeing inefficiencies and working to solve them. I was being rewarded with a permanent job and responsibility because of all the times I said, "What the hell?" (or in today's vernacular, "WTF?") It was not only that, though; it was because I took the responsibility to fix the problems I saw. This is where I learned one of the most important lessons of my entire career: *Problems that others saw as "the way its always been done" or as "the cost of doing business" should be questioned. Once investigated—and solved—these can open up big opportunities.*

Saying WTF—and feeling the frustration that comes with inefficiencies around the status quo—is not something that should annoy you, but rather something that should excite you. You should look at it as the first step to your next breakthrough.

MAKE TECH YOUR COMPETITIVE ADVANTAGE

Technology can be a game changer in every job and every industry. Eli Whitney's cotton gin, introduced in 1794, did in one hour what it took several people to do in a day. With this invention, cotton became America's leading crop. The invention of the first commercial steam engine in 1712 was by most accounts the technology that began the Industrial Revolution in England. From mines to mills, the introduction of steam engine technology improved productivity and provided a constant source of power to run trains, boats, and machines in factories. Prior to the steam engine, water was the primary supplier of power. Steam engines made it possible to expand the American West without having to worry about the presence of waterways and to establish communities that weren't geographically close to rivers and streams. It led to the creation of new towns, cities, and states. Any entrepreneur that can understand how a manual process can be automated now has the power and the engine to do so. It didn't take much to create an unfair competitive advantage when pitting a machine against manual labor.

We see examples like this throughout the centuries, throughout the globe. In 1911 the precursor to IBM was formed as the Computing-Tabulating-Recording Company (CTR). This tabulating machine was in essence the first very rudimentary computer. More than an adding machine, it took in punch cards with various pieces of information and added and recorded multiple bits of information. Its earliest use was to conduct population censuses in countries around the world and then provide cross-referenced data such as the number of people within a city based on gender or age. This type of computation could never have been done before. It wasn't long before businesses got wind of what these machines could do and began adopting them to provide early data processing to keep track of sales and revenue and provide data back by salesperson, product, and more. If a company could now mine data more readily to see which products are selling well and which are not, which salespeople are bringing in revenue and which are not, they would have an unfair competitive advantage in managing their business.

We can fast-forward to the use of technology by a company like Uber, which built a global company around a mobile application that makes it easier and provides better information around calling for a car service. This is not a problem that people knew they had in an industry that most thought could not be disrupted. For cities with little or no taxi system, it provides people with the ability to leave their cars at home and know that they can still get from one place to the next. For anyone who travels, it's nice to have one app that you can use to access a car or a taxi in major cities around the United States and the world.

The pace of technology change is increasing, and technology itself is becoming cheaper and faster to develop. This simply means that a company that used technology to disrupt the status quo can themselves be disrupted by applying new technologies. Sony created the first portable music player, known as the Walkman. It introduced the Discman when CDs came out and an early MP3 player as well. It was Apple that paired the MP3 player (iPod) with a music download service (iTunes), making it simple to fill the MP3 player with music of your choice. With that, Sony went from creating and owning the mobile music player market to no longer being a player in the market.

Blockbuster used the VCR and videotapes to create a national chain of stores. Netflix created a mail order DVD company with no physical presence and then disrupted their own business model, when broadband became ubiquitous, with a Web-based streaming video. Blockbuster is out of business. Netflix is thriving.

Who do you want to be? Understand that with the pace of technological change, the disruptor can easily become the disrupted. Positive destruction must be constant.

Notes

1. John Holusha, "W. Edwards Deming, Expert on Business Management, Dies at 93." *New York Times,* December 21, 1993; www.nytimes.com/1993/12/21/obituaries/w-edwards-deming-expert-on-business-management-dies-at-93.html

2. Mark Magnier, "Rebuilding Japan with the Help of 2 Americans." *Los Angeles Times,* October 25, 1999; articles.latimes.com/1999/oct/25/news/ss-26184

3. Junji Noguchi, "The Legacy of W. Edwards Deming." *Quality Progress* 28(12) (October 1995): 35–38.

4. Deming's 1950 lecture to Japanese management. Translation by Teruhide Haga; hclectures.blogspot.com/1970/08/demings-1950-lecture-to-japanese.html

5. *Deming of America* (Documentary) (Cincinnati, OH: The Petty Consulting/Productions, 1991); priscillapetty.com/page7/page7.html

6. www.deming.org/theman/theories/fourteenpoints

7. Holusha, 1993.

8. www.nytimes.com/1993/12/21/obituaries/w-edwards-deming-expert-on-business-management-dies-at-93.html?pagewanted = 2

9. Holusha, 1993.

10. R. Dan Reid and Nada R. Sanders. *Operations Management* (Hoboken, NJ: John Wiley & Sons, 2013), Chapter 5: Total Quality Management; www.wiley.com/college/sc/reid/chap5.pdf

11. Patrick Vlaskovitz, "Henry Ford, Innovation and That Faster Horse Quote." *Harvard Business Review,* April 29, 2011; hbr.org/2011/08/henry-ford-never-said-the-fast/

12. Ibid.
13. Andrea Gabor, "Ford Embraces Six-Sigma Quality Goals." *New York Times,* June 13, 2001; www.nytimes.com/2001/06/13/business/13QUAL.html
14. Mark Milian, "14 Years Later, Dell Founder Backtracks on Apple Attack." CNN .com, October 18, 2011; www.cnn.com/2011/10/18/tech/web/michael-dell-apple/
15. Ari Levy, "Google Parent Alphabet Passes Apple Market Cap at the Open." CNBC, February 2, 2016; www.cnbc.com/2016/02/01/google-passes-apple-as-most-valuable-company.html
16. Milian, 2011.
17. Eric Newcomer, "Venture Funding of U.S. Startups Last Year Was Most since 2000." Bloomberg.com, January 16, 2015; www.bloomberg.com/news/articles/2015-01-16/it-s-official-startup-funding-last-year-was-biggest-since-2000
18. Tim Bowler, "Falling Oil Prices: Who Are the Winners and Losers?" BBC News, January 19, 2015; www.bbc.com/news/business-29643612

PART

2

LEADING THE INNOVATION

3

Create an Unfair Competitive Advantage

After six months in Israel, working as a cook on a kibbutz and keeping up with financial news through the editions of the *Wall Street Journal* my father Fed Ex-ed me, I returned to Wall Street. But it wasn't the same place I left. Although I thought I'd be diving right back into the risk arbitrage department, I found that everything at Oppenheimer was different. The firm had been sold and risk arbitrage spun off to be its own entity, now called Junction Partners.

For me, the upshot of the change was that I was the recipient of a promotion. I became an assistant trader at 22 years old. I continued to be driven by my passion to make the operations more efficient, and this time, in this new firm, my ideas were well received.

Management was interested in improving efficiency with new technologies, and I started working with computer consultants to automate the calculation of the spreads for every deal, which would give us an unfair competitive advantage. I built spreadsheets and put in data such as "probability of completion and date of close" so we could get probability-based annualized returns and sort the best opportunities. These things were just common sense to me. And although this introduced new methods and practices that required changes, everyone was open to adopting them because they gave us such an edge.

The following year was marked by a bigger transformation—technology was now viewed as invaluable, and adopting it was a company-wide imperative. The CEO delivered a presentation to the investors on the firm's goals to amplify the level of automation. He included a slide that had a mandate for the number of computers in the firm and the number of people to be 2:1. There was only one computer in the office just a year before.

With the new directive, we all fully embraced the PC. We leveraged the power of computing to track stock quotes and run analytics. Deals went from paper to the screen. We now gained the ability to calculate spreads in real time and were able to find more opportunities to invest profitably and make more money. Automating this process gave us a very clear, unfair competitive advantage.

WHAT IS AN UNFAIR COMPETITIVE ADVANTAGE?

There are many variables in a business, whether a start-up or an established company, that are beyond anyone's control. You have to figure out what you can control and make sure you control it and how you can stack the deck in your favor over the competition.

The most important thing is to create a company, a product, or a service that within 30 seconds of a pitch, a prospective client will understand your unfair competitive advantage; why it is so much better, cheaper, or more efficient. It should be so compelling that they would be stupid not to buy it and if it is a business service that you are creating, if their competitor bought it and they did not, they would be at a disadvantage. This is your unique selling proposition (USP).

Two years later, at 24 years old, I became head trader. It was not because I was a great trader or even because of my ideas to increase efficiency. It was because my immediate boss, who had reported to the head of the firm for 14 years, asked for a raise, which instigated an argument and resulted in my boss getting fired. I didn't get fired because I was making $25,000 a year and therefore not exactly putting a dent in the company coffers.

While being head trader sounds like a dream gig, it didn't turn out to be such a coup. In fact, it was awful. Instead of being able to do more from my new post, I was more penned in than ever. The head of the firm was a forward thinker in that he loved the idea of automation, but he also came from the more traditional command-and-control school of management, which made him difficult to work for.

I was miserable. I lamented that I was able to be more creative when I was not in the spotlight. Now, I had to report everything to my boss, and I couldn't get him to agree to anything. Every idea I had was "stupid." Everything I brought up, he shot down.

There weren't that many hedge fund managers at the time, and most of them had terrible reputations as people managers. Making so much money yielded a sense of entitlement; they saw themselves as the ones making money and everyone else as costing them money. As a result, some treated people incredibly poorly. I found the environment to be debilitating, and it turned me off from ever wanting to work for anyone else ever again. I swore that if I ever had my own firm, I would never run it that way. It was formative—almost like having abusive parents and swearing one day you'd be the exact opposite kind of parent.

My frustration built up over six months until I couldn't take the day-to-day insults. I went to his office and quit. He accepted my resignation. Amazingly, he then asked me to continue in a different capacity, working as an independent consultant to collaborate with the computer consultants and advise them on the business aspects we needed to automate. There was still a huge divide between people who understood the business and people who understood technology and I could serve as that bridge. For this, he offered me more than I was paid as an employee. I didn't have any better opportunities lined up, so I accepted the offer.

Stacking the Deck

At this time, trading still worked in a rather convoluted way, and this backward process still confounded me. A trader picked up the phone to call a broker with a symbol and a number of shares to buy or sell, and as the trade was executed, the trader would write down how much was traded. Sometimes the whole trade went through and it was very straightforward. Other times, it was more complicated, with traders having to prorate different amounts and write tickets for every account managed. Those tickets had to be keypunched into multiple systems such as the accounting and clearing systems. As you'd imagine, there were often mistakes made with manual input into multiple systems. Traders blamed the people entering the data and vice versa. Everything was reconciled the next day, and mistakes were corrected. But this is how things had been done for years and likely how they were going to continue.

But I saw an opportunity—something that if done right could give investment firms a significant edge. I proposed creating an automated order management system (OMS) that could run on computers. The OMS would track this information automatically and provide up-to-the-minute data. I initially called it the Paperless

Trading System. I pitched it to my old boss, saying traders and portfolio managers were doing far too much clerical work and computers could do a better job. While he once thought all of my ideas were stupid, he liked this one right away. "Yeah, let's do it," he said.

My former boss saw in the OMS the ability to use technology to grow assets without growing staff. In Chapter 1 we saw how Cemex stacked the deck by innovating with a "just-in-time" system that enabled efficiencies and cut costs. We also saw how Dell stacked the deck with the same strategy that allowed it to compete on price and flexibility and win. Apple stacked the deck with its music player. It was not the first to come to that party. In fact, it was quite late. But it stacked the deck by coupling the music player with its own platform to download and access music easily. With that, it instantly owned the music player and digital music markets. In another example, as Amazon grew from selling books to selling everything, it needed a way to stack the deck in its favor and it found it with its annual subscription program Amazon Prime. The big problem it had to overcome was competing against brick-and-mortar retailers that offered customers the instant gratification of leaving the store with the item. By combining its huge selection with the ability for customers to receive the item the next day for no additional cost, Amazon minimized this issue and forever changed retail.

AUTOMATION IS THE PREREQUISITE TO INFORMATION BEING POWER

Specifically, the OMS was attractive to my former boss, and later to other customers, because it created leverage to scale assets without adding head count. It also produced better and more real-time data so the traders and portfolio managers could focus on investments and spend less time on clerical tasks. All of this produced more profits—and that created an unfair competitive advantage for those who implemented our OMS over those who did not.

We've seen many other companies in a myriad of other industries win with this tactic of enabling automation. Perhaps the best example comes from Walmart. In retail the common mantra for achieving success is "location, location, location." But Sam Walton, the king of retail himself, had a different theory. Walton said it was all about information—accessing information quickly and knowing what to do with it—that helped enable Walmart to become the world's largest retailer.

In 1983, long before the Internet made data readily available more broadly and cheaply, Walton set up a private satellite system to track delivery trucks, process credit card transactions, and transmit sales data. It cost $24 million to build—a sizable investment at the time—and the results were not immediately evident.[1] But soon, this satellite system proved a tremendous competitive advantage.

The system had a 65-week rolling history of every single item stocked. With that, Walmart could look at any item—a TV, a red sweater, a grill—and see exactly how many it stocked and how many it sold, not only overall, but in every region, every district, and every store. That led the company to pioneer "just-in-time inventory," eliminating the need for storage at each store. With this system, the local distribution center would know when a store was nearly out of product and could send more in immediately.[2] As Walton wrote in his book, *Made in America*, "We've always known that information gives you a certain power, but the degree to which we can retrieve it in our computer really does give us the power of competitive advantage."[3]

The satellite system became the largest civilian database of its kind in the world.[4] It also catapulted Walmart to become the largest retailer, leapfrogging the large chains it once tried to compete against. It made Sam Walton and his family among the richest people in the world. It also changed the way retail operated—it provided such an edge that every retailer has since adopted point-of-sale systems so they can actively mine data for better inventory management and in real time know what's selling and what's not.

Getting Started on My Own

Although I was grateful that I had this consulting gig, it wasn't really what I had intended on doing when I quit Junction Partners. I wasn't thinking about starting my own financial software firm. I liked working on deals and had been scouring for jobs in corporate finance at various financial institutions.

Merrin Financial—the name I had given my consultancy—was just me working in the back of Dad's gallery with a computer, an answering machine, and some business cards.

I gained clients one by one. During my search for a job, someone at Soros, the massive hedge fund, heard what I was doing with computer systems at Junction and asked me to come in and meet with them. (Junction was affiliated with Odyssey, one of the largest hedge funds at time, and all of the big hedge fund managers spoke to one another.)

I was 24 years old and found myself in the same room as the legendary George Soros, explaining the benefits of my proposed OMS to him. I was sweating profusely, but he was really nice, and as expected, he was really intelligent. Soros had a lot of questions, but it was obvious that he clearly saw the benefit of automating the trading aspects of his business. After that meeting, they asked me to come on as a consultant.

Around the same time, I met a renowned hedge fund manager, who was having lunch with his wife at my parents' country house north of New York City. I was visiting, and as they were leaving I asked them if they could give me a lift back to the city. I recognized this as an opportunity I couldn't pass up. It was a calculated move, as I would have them as a captive audience for the whole hour back. I was sitting in the backseat of the car and the wife asked what I was doing for a living. After I finished explaining the concept of the OMS, she said to her husband, "Don't you need something like this?"

It wasn't that my pitch was perfect; in fact, I wasn't really pitching them at all. This was a one-hour conversation about what I was up to with my parents' friend. I won her sympathy.

I never would have been successful selling this hedge fund manager directly, but because of his wife's insistence, he asked me to come in the next day, and soon after, he too engaged me as a computer consultant. None of this was what I planned on doing, but I was making money and too busy to think about searching for employment in mergers and acquisitions or corporate finance.

When, finally, I received a full-time job offer, I was so entrenched in my consulting activities that I turned it down. It was an easy decision, actually. There was a wide-open field to explore, and working for myself was much more exciting.

BEING THE FIRST IS ONE WAY TO STACK THE DECK

Educating the marketplace, creating demand, and removing friction for a new idea takes time. With Merrin Financial it took us five years for the OMS platform to go mainstream and be adopted by the industry. (All time spans have since collapsed due to the Internet.) It's hard work to introduce a new idea, but the payoff can be worth it: the first mover often gets the advantage.

While no advantage can last forever, we've seen that the companies that build first-mover advantages can dominate their product categories for many years. Coca-Cola, Hoover, Gillette, Oracle, Microsoft, and IBM all won market share from their respective market's beginning to its maturity.[5]

Now, Uber is enjoying the benefits of being first and is the dominant player in the multibillion global ride-sharing sector it started.[6] It dominates because of scale and switching costs (most customers stay with what's working and what they are comfortable with). It's also succeeding because of the head start it had as a digital marketplace that connects buyers and sellers. Network effects allow Uber to get bigger as consumers flock to the services with the most providers.

Uber has had to work tirelessly to educate consumers and take on the taxi industry and battle regulatory issues, but it's paid off. The entire U.S. taxi industry is worth far less than Uber's valuation.[7] Its closest competitor, Lyft, still lags far behind.[8] And, on paper, it's one of the world's largest transportation companies—more valuable than Hertz, Avis, United Airlines, and General Motors.[9]

Learning on the Job Is One Way to Do It . . .

Now that I had a few clients interested in the OMS, I had to figure out how to build it. Every time a new client signed on, I was euphoric and then I was scared senseless. "Oh, s!#t, what do I do now" was the refrain of the time.

I didn't know the first thing about where to start. I didn't have a business plan or a budget, nor did I understand sales or how to build a technology product. After all, I hadn't exactly excelled in that one computer course I registered for at Tufts.

My biggest problem was that I didn't have any kind of business plan. I was just drifting from one consulting project to another. I liked the projects and found them rewarding, but none of them were the kinds of projects that could be rinsed and repeated.

Consider the work I did with Laura Sloate, a legendary investment manager who has been blind since she was 6 years old. Laura, an investor in Junction Partners, had someone read all of the financial reports and newspapers to her, but she craved more independence and asked me to help build a technology that could read everything to her. There was some existing technology that could read to you in the 1980s, so I took that and worked with people from quote systems and news services to hook those up and have it read aloud. With this, Laura could enter stock quotes and hear how they were doing, and she could listen to news stories, delivered in computerized voices, which she could speed up and slow down. It provided her a whole new level of independence.

In another one-off project, I helped my parents' neighbor, Bill Jacobs, who had a reinsurance company, to utilize new online services to access data he needed about companies he was insuring. (This was years before the Internet we know today). I thought a lot about how to structure the service, but I hadn't thought a lot about how to structure the pricing.

"How much will this consulting project cost?" Bill asked, excited about the solution I was offering.

"A thousand dollars," I said.

We were in a group of people and he asked me to leave the room with him.

"For $1,000 it's not worth anything," he said. "You should charge $10,000 and people will take it seriously."

That was a lot of money, especially considering that I had no clue what I was doing, but I realized not only was he right, but also that doing bespoke custom work was not building long-term value and not what I wanted to do.

Price Right

A very common mistake made by many first-time entrepreneurs is underpricing their service. At least that's what happened to me— twice. I priced my solution too low for Bill Jacobs's data project, and I did it again when coming up with how to price the OMS. But I learned my lesson fast and figured out not just how much to charge but, more importantly, a new pricing strategy.

The OMS wasn't ready for launch yet, but we couldn't wait until it was finished to start marketing it. We knew the sales cycle would be long—perhaps six months—so we needed to start selling it in advance. You can't wait until a product is perfectly packaged to start selling it; you start selling it when it's close to being ready.

But that meant we needed to determine a price when we still had no idea about our costs. All of the variables we needed to establish a pricing structure were still unknown: How many would we sell? How much would it take to support the product? How much did it cost to sell the product?

I didn't know how much to sell it for, but I did know I didn't want to start every year with the same hurdle over my head to have to make more sales each year to grow the business. Besides, with the OMS, we were introducing a new type of software, and it would be a hard sell because the market didn't know yet that it needed it. I didn't want to just sell it for a fixed fee, so we came up with a new model for software, one that charged an ongoing monthly fee. Charging a monthly fee—which was much less in the short term than a large up-front payment, but which would be charged in perpetuity—would grow our revenue with each new account and could be increased as we added new features, modules—and users. While we would make less money up front, building a recurring revenue model was attractive from both a cash flow and enterprise value perspective. Today, of course, this "subscription model" is commonly used for software, but it was not done at the time.

It was a smart idea—and one that later gave us a much needed lifeline for survival—but initially we priced the product too cheaply, charging $1,000 a month. We had no idea what it would take to support and maintain these systems, nor did we know how many systems we would sell. We soon learned that we had to do a lot of customization for each account. We kept the monthly recurring charge, which was the right strategy, but we found a way to fix the wrong price we had set by charging consulting and customization fees. With that, we were able to build more functionality into the product with someone else paying for its development.

As our product progressed, we added more functionality, we added more clients and references, and the market started understanding that it needed this service. We were able to increase pricing every year. We also broke the product into different modules such as domestic and international equities, and compliance. We charged different amounts for the different modules and added a per-user fee. Our pricing offered our customers the elasticity to add services and seats as they went, and that flexibility made us a more attractive offering.

But everyone's pricing was the same. We stayed away from doing special deals because I never wanted my existing clients to feel that someone else got a better deal. It also made every negotiation much easier. We raised our prices over time as we increased our feature set, and we didn't bundle special packages that favored one client over another.

The enterprise software company Salesforce, which was founded later and built on a subscription model, also found that pricing mechanism to be a key differentiator. Salesforce helped pioneer "Software as a Service," offering its users the opportunity to use its software without the customary up-front investment costs required to buy, implement, and maintain the software. The service grew virally. It was so inexpensive that users were able to get started by just purchasing it on their credit cards, without having to get approval from their department heads. And once they were on it, they found it invaluable and Salesforce had an "in," which allowed it to execute its "land and expand" strategy.

Out of Control

In an effort to grow the business into something with a little more structure, I teamed up with Richard Stein, a friend I had met in summer camp when I was a teenager. The first thing Rich did was balance my checkbook and untangle the mess I made. I'd been paying business expenses out of my personal checkbook and not doing a great job of separating my personal and corporate accounts.

We moved into our first office—an 800-square-foot space in a very old building on Fifth Avenue in New York City. Rich and I shared an office. Our office was so small that we couldn't close the door and we shared one desk. I sat at the desk and he sat at the return. Both of us couldn't get up at same time. One day, a mouse fell from the ceiling onto a computer keyboard.

We used a coffee machine that must have been in the office for years before we got there. We didn't think to clean it and the coffee came out green. We were so tired and cheap, we drank it anyway. There were probably five years of mouse droppings in it. I look back and wonder how I could be so stupid and how we are still alive.

Even more stupid, developing the OMS took far longer than I anticipated—and promised. I had set unrealistic expectations. Not only did I have zero experience developing software, but we were creating a new product category that had no road map or fully defined feature set. I told our clients that we would have it built in six months.

After one year of waiting for the product, my three clients, especially my old boss at Junction Partners, were getting restless. We were constantly under the gun and getting grilled, "Where is it? What's happening? Why isn't it done yet?"

We had started in 1985. We delivered the first OMS to Junction in the middle of 1987—about one and a half years after I said I would deliver it.

It was a typical Version 1 product with all the bugs, and made worse because we didn't know anything about version control or how to package for distribution. It was a massive amount of work to implement the product because we had to integrate it with so many other systems. We had not anticipated how complicated this would be or the differences in trading styles within each firm. We had to keep track of different securities with different rules. Clients had different commission rates. There were different allocation methodologies. It was challenging to customize the software for every client and at the same time try to sell the OMS to new potential clients.

Beyond Your Control

Then, all of those issues took a backseat to something beyond our control. The stock market crashed in October 1987, just a few months after we launched. It suddenly became impossible to sell the OMS at all. It was an entirely different climate. No one knew if they would stay in business. The mood was so extreme that many likened it to the stock market crash of 1929 all over again. People thought the world would end.

The only good news was that we did not lose the clients we had. The reason: once they started using our service, they would never go back to the old, manual way. The computerized system was so much more efficient than the paper-based system, and it was able to provide valuable data in real time. We could calculate so many things: you could see real-time positions, profit and loss, and whether you had enough cash to buy more stock.

Let me walk you through an example. Let's say a portfolio manager decides he likes a stock and he wants it to represent 3 percent of his portfolio. If he manages a $100 million portfolio, he would buy $3 million worth of that stock. That ultimately has to be translated into a number of shares for the trader to buy. The OMS could figure that out instantly. Now, that's not a hard example, but let's say he wanted it to be 3.5 percent of the portfolio and he managed $147 million. And then you have to consider the complicating factors: suppose he already owns 1.5 percent and manages 10 different accounts and wants to bring all of the accounts up to a 3.5 percent position. The stock is trading at $22 a share. How many shares does he have to buy across all accounts? The portfolio manager or trader would have to spend time on this equation, but the OMS calculated it instantly.

It also kept track of everything, from what was ordered to what was completed, what remained to be bought or sold, and eventually all the regulatory and compliance requirements. Paper tickets could not do those calculations or keep track of any of this.

Once you have that kind of capability, you can never go back to paper and pen. It's like Quicken®. Before Quicken came around, you wrote checks in your checkbook and you had to reconcile everything at the end of the month. You did not have any analysis, you could not produce reports that showed you "rent is 30% of expenses" or "you spent more on groceries this month than you did last month" or "one of your children is spending twice as much as the other children on her phone plan." But now that we have that, would you ever go back to writing checks? Being able to provide this kind of leap in efficiency stacks the deck for your customers and for you.

IT'S NOT ALL ABOUT TIMING

There's a lot of talk about timing. There's a lot written about the great companies that were started in dire economic times: General Electric, Southwest Airlines, Salesforce. Marc Benioff, Salesforce's CEO, has cited the Eskimo proverb, "The storm is the time to fish," when talking about doing business in times of economic uncertainty.[10]

My timing has always left something to be desired. But here's the thing: people who start businesses do not wait for cycles of recession or cycles of growth; they just start companies because they are compelled to solve a big problem.

It doesn't matter what type of cycle you start it in. But it might matter how you tell your message.

- **In a recession:** Focus on how to save costs.

- **In a period of growth:** Focus on how your product or service can help accelerate sales or revenues.

The most important thing in both scenarios is to have enough money in the bank to keep the company growing until sales take off.

By 1989, we had a total of seven clients. We were not growing, and we were not profitable. Between the state of the financial markets and educating the hard-to-change mind-set of status quo, we were hurting. Badly. We had no structure around the growth of the company or the management of technology, the quality of the software was poor, and we were constantly being yelled at by clients.

One day, I was with a customer installing a new version of the software. It was full of bugs and the lead programmer was on the telephone, on speakerphone, so the whole room of people could hear the conversation as he was running me through what I had to do. The software would not work and he got so frustrated that he announced that he was quitting on speakerphone in front of our client, leaving me high and dry without a working system and with no clue how to fix it. That was just how it went in those days. We lurched from one problem to the next, and every day seemed like a new low.

Rich and I took a walk around the block and had an honest and unsettling conversation.

"If we don't see any light at the end of six months, we'll have to close shop," Rich said.

We were half a year away from having to shut down. Six months came and went, and if I had known how to file for bankruptcy, I would have. But I didn't. (That's how clueless I was.) I don't recommend this but sometimes ignorance can work in your favor. Not knowing how to declare bankruptcy is what ultimately gave us the time we needed to have the business take off. A certain amount of ignorance is also why so many outsiders succeed at reinventing businesses and industries. They are not mired in the status quo or how things are typically done and, therefore, might bring different solutions to the common problems. Some ignorance is also necessary in starting a business. I've heard countless times from entrepreneurs that if they had known how hard it would be to start or build their business, they never would have started.

THE NUMBER ONE REASON THAT START-UPS FAIL IS RUNNING OUT OF MONEY

What dooms most start-ups is running out of cash. My family acted as my venture capitalist, and if they had not continued to help me fund my payroll, I would have been out of business. I didn't know about other options like venture capital, which was not as prominent then as it is now. Nor was I confident about taking someone else's money and putting it into the business. My dad was incredibly generous, but not everyone has that luxury.

I made lots of mistakes as I learned on the job. I was able to learn on the job because of my special circumstances. In my next business I tried not to repeat those mistakes. I created business and marketing plans; I figured out how to stack the deck in my favor as best as I could. I marketed to my previous clients, and I decided that I would raise capital and use someone else's money to fund the business—that's a deal I would do again every time.

But the reality of being a first-time entrepreneur is that investment from friends and family is the way most companies initially get off the ground. However, you must exercise caution. These days, a lot of people come to me looking for funding for their idea for an app. Some of the ideas are great and some are just complete crap. But, overall, there are some very unrealistic expectations. In today's world, everybody knows somebody who got rich quick, or they've read about Mark Zuckerberg, Steve Jobs, or Bill Gates never graduating from college and they think they can do the same thing. But in reality, achieving this kind of success is no different than becoming a sports legend. Most basketball players are not Kobe Bryant. You can aspire to be, but the probability is that you will not get there.

Are you going to take money from friends and family? Follow these principles:

- Do your homework—create business and marketing plans.

- Be prepared—don't take other people's money before you validate your concept with prospective customers, listen and refine your concept with their input, define your unique selling proposition, and perfect your sales pitch.

- Be highly convinced this is an idea that can change the way business gets done.

- Make sure you have created an unfair competitive advantage for your customers and, therefore, for your business as well, so you can stack the deck in your favor.

- Hire the right people and build the right culture. (You either have a culture by design or a culture by default. More on this in Chapter 11.)

If You Fail to Plan, You Plan to Fail

Unaware of any other options, we kept on working on the OMS, making it better, faster, and adding necessary features. Just as important, my father helped me improve my own skill set and taught me the most important lessons of all—the value of serious preparation and how to sell. Maybe I didn't know all of the answers, but I surely could make myself more prepared and learn some sales skills and that would give me and the company a better chance of success.

This all started on a sailboat somewhere off the Greek Islands. Every year, my parents took us sailing, exploring a different part of the world, and this time we were on the Aegean Sea. I was completely depressed about what was happening at work. It was obvious that Merrin Financial was not going anywhere, and I had to come up with some way to fix it. But instead of getting mired in why people weren't buying the product (the market had tanked and people didn't think they needed it), Dad worked with me on finding solutions.

"You gotta be a great salesperson," he said.

That was easier said than done. I had no idea how to do this. Unlike my father or my brother Sam, I was not a natural salesperson. I was a terrible salesperson with a bad attitude toward selling. I felt that if someone were stupid enough to not buy my product pretty much on the spot, they were too stupid for me to call again. My selling skills and attitude had to change for me to succeed. Despite my attitude, it was not enough to make Dad give up on me.

"Pitch me," he said. He would pretend to be the customer: "Why should I buy this? What good will it do me?"

I pitched to him. I was bad.

"Too long!" said Dad.

"You didn't give the benefits!" said my brother Sam.

"You didn't nail it," Dad said.

It wasn't easy hearing how much I sucked, but that was okay because they gave me pointers. "You have 30 seconds to make them understand why they need to buy it, or you haven't done enough work," Dad told me.

He was right. I hadn't done enough work. Most people do not do enough work. I pitched constantly for the entire trip. By the time I got back, I was actually pretty good and learned incredibly valuable lessons about selling, preparation, and role-playing. I became so enthusiastic about the success of practicing through role-playing that I have made it a key part of all our sales training and even developed a negotiation strategy around it that I called the 3×3 that we'll discuss in Chapter 8.

I learned a pivotal lesson in pitching from Dad and in the years since I've learned that perfecting a pitch is a continuous process. Today, every time we start a new product or launch a new line of business, I like to go on the pitches because it's an opportunity to learn what resonates and what doesn't. For example, if we hear the same questions more than a few times, we know we need to work it into the pitch and answer it before they ask it.

CONSTANTLY PERFECT YOUR PITCH OVER TIME

A good pitch is constantly refined and redefined. There are a few things to look for to help you modify your pitch and make it more impactful:

- Commonly asked questions: What are people asking about? This reveals need-to-know information. Work it into your pitch earlier.

- A change in circumstances or change in the environment: As new products enter the market and there's a new hot thing du jour, you should change your pitch to incorporate what is relevant to the day, to the specific customer, and to the unique opportunity. For example, when we saw a technology change and peer-to-peer computing became big, we incorporated it more heavily into the pitch. Today, we are seeing huge regulatory changes in Europe, so we include how our product enables customers to comply with the new regulations into the pitch.

- Study your audience. If we did our homework and knew a customer needed greater operational efficiency, that's what we pitched to them.

- Use the most current statistics as proof points to increase credibility. We use statistics any way we can. At Merrin Financial we added all of the assets of every client so we were able to say "$100 billion of assets now being managed using Merrin Financial." We also sliced it in other ways, saying "We have 4 of the top 10 leading asset managers on our system." When working in a new product category, it's especially important to give people a level of comfort that this is not bleeding edge but that this is going into the mainstream. You want to demonstrate that firms like theirs are signing up and by waiting longer they could be at a disadvantage. Add every big win to your pitch.

Sell, Sell, Sell

With my new selling skills semi-mastered, I gained the confidence to reach out to a potential giant customer. I also used Dad's advice to "leverage any opportunity."

This was exactly how we won over Michael Price, one of world's most lauded value investors at that time. Michael ran Heine Securities and the Mutual Series set of mutual funds. I sent him a letter, unsolicited.

I knew that he knew my old boss. I introduced myself, and wrote about how Merrin Financial did all of Junction Partners' computer systems. I wrote that I had a system that I thought he would be interested in.

Just a few days later I received a call from his assistant, inviting me to come to his office downtown. The office was not what I expected. There was only one old computer in the entire place. I did a demo on my laptop with the whole firm crowded around. Then, Michael walked in and asked, "Which one of you is Seth Merrin?"

I thought it was strange for him not to be able to identify me, as everyone else worked for him, but I wasn't about to say anything that could get me on his bad side. "That would be me," I replied.

"You did all of Junction's computer systems?" he asked.

"Yes," I responded.

And that was it. It was the easiest sales pitch ever, and Michael Price signed on and became our biggest customer. This very large new account would serve as a pivotal endorsement. Where we were once six months away from going out of business, we began to experience an exciting turnaround. As the 1980s ended and a new decade began, it seemed that people's mind-set changed: investors started to believe that the world wasn't coming to an end. And Merrin Financial was given a second chance.

We saw the value of hard work and the returns it could bring. We had brought on a few more clients and spent the past two years enhancing the product, and now people wanted it. We ended the decade with a total of seven clients and 20 employees. In 1990 we signed 18 new clients, and Merrin Financial braced for rapid growth.

We moved from the terrible mouse-infested building to a bigger office vacated by a garment showroom. We couldn't afford movers, so we put everything on office chairs and rolled them down Fifth Avenue a few blocks away.

That year we hit an inflection point and our system became a MUST-have. We held on for dear life. It was a confluence of events; we hired better salespeople, and we built enough functionality to satisfy the needs of more clients and minimize the amount of customization needed. We added clients and employees, and we had to move again.

We made progress with big companies, including getting very close to finalizing a deal with the asset management arm of a Fortune 500 company. They wanted to see our office. The new place was better than the rodent hotels and garment showrooms, but it was still a dump. The weekend before the meeting, we went to Ikea and bought furniture and had everyone come in and assemble it. We also had to paint the place. I felt like we were building a stage. By Monday it looked presentable. I was a bit worried they would smell wet paint or the furniture would collapse.

We were such a little company; this prospect was coming in to kick the tires. The tires were not even bolted onto the car! Still, somehow, they liked what they saw and they became our next major milestone client. We had customers that managed tens of billions of dollars. They managed hundreds of billions of dollars.

Now, we had a new head of sales and hired additional salespeople. We had new products for international trading and compliance. We had amazing references, such as Michael Price, who stated that he went from $2 billion to $20 billion—which he said he couldn't have done without Merrin Financial. We also evolved from the narrow scope of being for the equity desks to serving fixed-income, foreign exchange, and portfolio managers.

My first five years creating the OMS were marked by my having to convince companies that they needed this product. But, eventually, the industry fully adopted this system as the central hub of information flow. Portfolio managers could connect to traders and traders could connect to the back office—all electronically. The entire investment process for capital markets could be conducted electronically without the need for manual intervention; the OMS became the spinal cord of these firms. I was invited to speak at conferences designed around this whole idea I invented. Today, the industry calls it straight-through processing (STP), and companies pay hundreds of thousands or millions of dollars a year for their OMS systems.

Our sales took off and we hired more experienced people, who put in better processes and quality control. We stabilized our business and grew to create an industry that enabled the start of the electronic trading era because we provided a solution that gave our clients a much better way to manage their business, which gave us an unfair competitive advantage and we didn't quit.

You have to have 100 percent conviction to get you through the ups and downs of a start-up, and if you don't, you should probably get out of it. I knew absolutely this was the way Wall Street had to go. Money was flowing into the industry, and our customers were growing quickly. Our OMS would help them manage their growth much more efficiently, with better information, fewer errors, and fewer people, and help avoid any compliance issues. We were selling companies an unfair competitive advantage—and they needed that. I knew this was going to happen, it was just a question of whether we would make it happen or if it would be someone else. Why shouldn't it be us?

STACKING THE DECK POSTMORTEM

What I did wrong and what I learned for next time

When we first started Merrin Financial, we were missing several ingredients I now know are essential to stack the deck. If I could do it again, I would ensure that I had these on my side. These things will increase your likelihood of success:

- Have enough money in the bank to last until sales kick in.

- Make sure you create an unfair competitive advantage for your customers and ultimately for your company.

- Define your unique selling proposition (USP); perfect your sales pitch and be able to deliver it within 30 seconds.

- Hire the right people and let them do their jobs. (We will explore people and culture in the coming chapters.)

Notes

1. Sam Walton, *Made in America* (New York, NY: Random House, 1993), 271; books.google.com/books?id=ggN9Kp8UVfwC&pg=PA271&lpg=PA271&dq=s-am+walton+and++systems&source=bl&ots=sbEl1RmBQX&sig=Pq3KtLQ-L5 G9z2QNfPeYbRambko&hl=en&sa=X&ved=0CD0Q6AEwBmoVChMIxs3o7d-AyAIVh7QUCh2YsgQ1#v=onepage&q=sam%20walton%20and%20%20 systems&f=false
2. *The Encyclopedia of Arkansas History & Culture.* "Walton, Samuel Moore." www.encyclopediaofarkansas.net/encyclopedia/entry-detail.aspx?entryID=1792
3. Walton, 1993, p. 272.
4. Ibid.
5. Fernando Suarez and Gianvito Lanzolla. "The Half Truth of First Mover Advantage." *Harvard Business Review,* April 2005; hbr.org/2005/04/the-half-truth-of-first-mover-advantage
6. Johana Bhuiyan, "It's Already Over and Uber Has Won," *BuzzFeed,* February 20, 2015; www.buzzfeed.com/johanabhuiyan/its-already-over-and-uber-has-won#.irj2BdJPZ
7. "IBISWorld's Taxi and Limousine Services in the U.S.: Market Research Report," August 2015; www.ibisworld.com/industry/default.aspx?indid=1951
8. Bhuiyan, 2015.
9. Jeff Bercovici, "The Bear Case for Uber (Yes, There Is One)," *Forbes,* July 28, 2014.
10. Marc Benioff, *Behind the Cloud* (San Francisco, CA: Jossey-Bass, 2009), 258.

What Do I Do Now?

Sometimes things actually start to seem easy; you feel like you've made it. Maybe you even think you can stop to rest or at least take a moment to breathe. What I've learned is that you can never get too comfortable. Just when you think you're at the top of your game, something comes along and challenges your position.

Things were finally going well, and we had seven years of success under our belt in which we identified a need no one else had, established an industry, and enabled the shift from manual to electronic trading, then something happened that changed everything. Microsoft Windows came out, shifting from ASCII codes and green-screen computing to a graphical user interface (GUI), which completely changed how people interacted with the computer. This new generation of software was light years ahead of MS-DOS, the system on which our order management system (OMS) application was built. Before too long, customers wanted a new Windows application. We were not yet offering one and didn't have a solid plan to do so. We knew it would require a huge investment to completely rebuild our application on this new operating system. Competitors started entering our space—none of whom had any legacy systems to replace. They came out with new Windows-based applications. Their new product made ours look incredibly antiquated.

We hadn't faced any competition for seven years. Now we were in a fierce war with the shiny new things, and we weren't at all prepared for battle. Windows had been around for a few years, but the early releases were not-ready-for-prime-time, mission-critical applications. IBM also came out with an operating system called OS/2. We didn't know which to adopt; there wasn't a clear-cut decision. IBM was a much larger, competitive company back then, and Microsoft was fairly new. One of our largest clients backed OS/2 completely—much to its dismay years later as Windows evolved and completely cornered the market.

We said we would launch a new Windows product to meet the growing demand, but we didn't. We were making money but not enough to invest in completely rewriting our product for an entirely different operating system. Our sales stalled. Clients grew impatient.

Every day, I went into the office and wanted to hide under the table after every nasty phone call or every time someone came to me with a new problem. It was exhausting. I would walk home 15 blocks and stop halfway to wallow in my depression. At home I would ask myself: *What did I get myself into?* I became incredibly depressed.

But that kind of reaction would not solve anything. I knew what we had to do. We needed to completely rewrite the application, while at the same time supporting the products we had. It wasn't a choice. If we did not do this, we would go out of business.

It was incredibly expensive to go through a complete technology change and build a whole new product while keeping the existing one running. We knew we had to bite the bullet and create an entirely separate team to build a parallel product from scratch. Unlike the existing product, where the updated features were funded by existing customers, here we had to fund the entire development ourselves.

We had to continue to sell and customize the old system to keep the money flowing, but we were on a programming treadmill as each new feature we were being paid to add to the old system had to be programmed into the new product but totally at our cost. The more we enhanced the old system, the longer it took us to release the new one. It felt like we were chasing our own tail. It took three years to develop the new product, and it would take another three to get the product stable. It cost millions. We had the cash flow to cover it, but Merrin Financial's profitability went to zero.

The long development time gave our competitors an opportunity to grab a decent lead and sign up the bulk of new customers. It also ate up all of our profits for the next few years. But we had no choice. This would be an enormous investment, but the consequence of not doing it was financial life or death.

It's So Easy to Get Disrupted

We're hardly the only company to have our own disruptive idea disrupted. We've seen this happen time and again. A company is first to market only to be bested by new competitors that attract customers with a shiny updated offering free from all the constraints of legacy products. It's so easy for a company to lose its edge, especially in today's world where the cost of technology continues to decline and the time to market is so much faster. Once others see you have a successful business model, you can count on competition coming in with something cheaper, faster, or differentiated in some way.

Take Sony and its iconic Walkman. A German-Brazilian guy by the name of Andreas Pavel invented the "Stereobelt," a personal portable stereo audio cassette player in 1972. Sony came up with a royalty agreement and began selling it as the Walkman in Japan in 1979. It soon became one of the company's most successful products ever.[1] The Walkman was revolutionary; it changed how we listen to music—making it portable and personal. Sony continued selling iterations of the Walkman, and a host of portable music innovations from other companies followed—the MP3 player, iPod, and iPhone. What's important to note is that these new entries didn't change the original idea. They still made music portable and personal. But they did it differently; they used the latest technology to make it easier to access a wider variety of music. With this evolution they were able to completely replace the Walkman, which is no longer manufactured and found today only in attics, on eBay, or at the Museum of Obsolete Technology.

Another example is Digital Equipment Corporation, which was founded by MIT electronics engineers Kenneth Olsen and Harlan Anderson to build high-performance, low-cost computers—minicomputers—in an era of expensive and enormous mainframe computers. The company enjoyed a rapid rise and made it to the number two computer maker, right behind IBM, and even challenged Big Blue's most powerful mainframes.[2]

But it didn't keep that top position secure. In the 1990s it lost market share to Hewlett-Packard and Sun. Why? Both of those companies adopted newer technologies, specifically the nonproprietary UNIX operating system that made far more software applications available than what was on Digital's proprietary system. The market responded: Digital didn't make a profit between 1990 and 1995.[3] Compaq Computer bought Digital Equipment in 1998 to help it move into enterprise services and compete against IBM, but discontinued Digital's PC manufacturing. Compaq was then acquired by Hewlett-Packard and sold some of Digital's products, but under its own logo.

Or what about Atari, which started the home game console craze and brought us some of the most well-known games of all time, including Pong, Space Invaders, and Pac-Man. The company employed Steve Wozniack and Steve Jobs[4] and skyrocketed to success. Its console, called VCS, was the best-selling holiday gift in 1979, and that year it also released Asteroids, Atari's most successful game of all time. (It was so popular in arcades that operators had to install larger coin boxes to accommodate all of the money spent by players![5]) With its next game, Tempest, it pioneered multiple difficulty levels, and with the launch of Centipede, it built a large female fan base.[6] It became the fastest-growing U.S. company in history.[7]

Then in the early 1980s, Atari had a huge flop with its E.T. video game, which many publications labeled as the "worst video game of all time."[8] And it also had to contend with the crash of the video game market, resulting in a massive recession of the industry. Revenues that had peaked at $3.2 billion in 1983 fell to $100 million by 1985. *Time* Magazine as well as other publications said that video games were a fad destined to go the way of the pet rock.

But just then, when it all seemed to be over, Nintendo made its U.S. debut. Nintendo understood that stores were spooked by lackluster sales so they devised a new marketing strategy: It included a robot called ROB with the Nintendo Entertainment System and stores began selling it in the toy section. It sold over 30 million consoles, eventually topping out with 61 million. Nintendo became number 1; Sega, another post-Atari entry, was number 2; and Atari slid down to number 3.[9] Nintendo continued to innovate with the Game Boy and DS, but its console couldn't stay on top forever. New entries like Sony's PlayStation 2 and the XBOX started to best it. But Nintendo didn't want to end up like Atari—and because it continued to innovate and adopt new technology, it didn't. It launched the Wii in 2006, a new system that let gamers control the action on screen with their hands and body as opposed to only a controller. It was an immediate hit. It leapt to the top spot, and Nintendo's stock skyrocketed from $19 a share to more than $120 a share.[10] Atari? It went bankrupt.

More recently, we all witnessed the social network MySpace disrupting Friendster, only to be disrupted by Facebook. And we saw Google disrupting Yahoo, which disrupted Excite and other early search engines. Of course, it's not only tech companies. Disruption to the industry leader—and the category maker—can happen in any industry. Think about how the big box retailers disrupted the neighborhood stores. Barnes & Noble displaced the local bookstores, and then Amazon and e-readers disrupted Barnes & Noble. Blockbuster Video wiped out local video stores, and then Netflix came along and disrupted Blockbuster. Walmart destroyed downtown stores, but now Amazon is worth more than Walmart. These are ever continuing trends.

The Curse of the S Curve

What all of these businesses also demonstrate, and what we did, too, is the typical cycle of business—the S curve. The S curve describes a product's acceptance by the market over time. It starts slowly and takes time to get off the ground, but once it does, it quickly ramps up. Revenue then goes into hyper-drive, but it doesn't last for long. Sales stabilize as the product gets to saturation or maturity, and eventually revenue flattens out or declines.[11]

The concept of the S curve is easy to understand, but knowing where you are on the curve is very difficult. As companies enter their growth phase, all too often people start thinking trees grow to the sky. But they never do. History is littered with examples of companies blowing up after achieving great heights: Control Data Corp., Hewlett-Packard, and Tandem Computers were innovative tech companies that couldn't sustain their dominant positions. So were great retailers of old—Sears, Kmart, Gimbels, Alexander's. We see this in almost every industry throughout history.

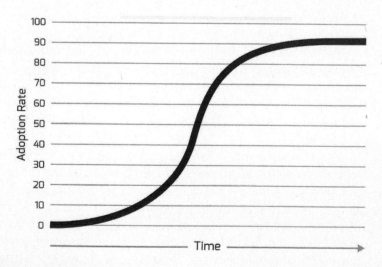

S-Curve Adoption Model

But, on the flip side, if you really perfect your understanding of the S curve, you introduce a new product at the right time during your S curve so revenue will not flatten out, but instead continue to grow. Apple became the best example of managing the S curve, certainly in recent history and perhaps of all time, after Steve Jobs returned to Apple in 1997. Apple went from a computer company with declining market share and margins to becoming a consumer products company and the most valuable company in the world.

Apple's product introduction timeline, when it started to effectively manage its S curve, is fascinating to analyze. Take a look at the time frames: it reveals that in order to create such bold new technologies and brand new product categories, Apple is constantly working on the next big thing.

2001—Apple introduces the iPod music player, kick-starting a whole new product category for Apple.

2003—The iTunes Store opens, allowing users to buy and download music, audiobooks, movies, and TV shows. The ability to cheaply and easily download music to the iPod further differentiates the iPod and sales take off.

2005—The iPod category adds product extensions of the lower-end iPod shuffle and iPod nano.

2007—Apple announces the iPhone smartphone, another new product category.

2008—Apple opens its App Store as an update to iTunes.

2009—Apple releases the iPhone 3GS, with more than twice the speed, improved performance, and a better camera with video capability and voice control.

2010—Apple begins selling the iPad tablet, another new product category, and gains an 84 percent share of the tablet market by year's end.

These innovations resulted in constant revenue increases for Apple, as you can see in the charts below. But strategizing right for the S curve is massively challenging. Almost every company in history has had to contend with it. And almost every company has gotten it wrong. It's endemic in the pharmaceutical industry. Every time a company has a blockbuster drug that goes off patent, it needs to have the next billion-dollar drug ready to go—but more often than not, it doesn't.

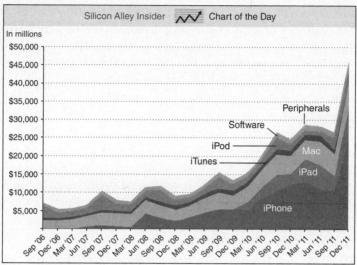

Source: Company filings (Jan. 24, 2012)

Apple's Revenue by Product

Source: Jay Yarrow and Kamelia Angelova, "Chart of the Day, The Evolution of Apple's Business." *Business Insider,* July 19, 2011; www.businessinsider.com/chart-of-the-day-apple-revenue-by-product-2011–7

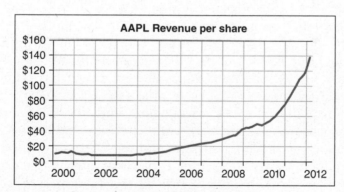

Extending the S Curve: Apple's Revenue from 2000 to 2012

Source: /static.cdn-seekingalpha.com/uploads/2012/2/20/863379–13297742350656683-Richard-Bloch.png

Companies must innovate continuously and map out the right strategy for the next big thing as soon as its latest launch is almost complete. When the initial launch gains traction is the right time to determine the next growth driver. Anything later is too late, as it always takes time for new products to gain traction. To time it perfectly, the new product's revenue has to grow faster than the old product's revenues decline.

I've found the biggest impediment to managing the S curve in my companies and others is the reluctance of the business managers to want to focus or invest in anything other than the biggest opportunity right in front of them, which is both correct and critical. *They* have to be focused on executing the current growth strategy for their business line. But the fact is that every new big opportunity can take years to validate, incubate, execute, and grow the revenue to the point that it can take over as the growth engine from the product or products that are maturing. When you see your growth slowing, it's too late to begin to invest in your new new thing. All too often, a company is faced with a flattening or declining growth curve, and it is at that point that it tends to make a "transformational acquisition," an acquisition designed to greatly diversify revenue or add a new business segment or technology designed to quickly jump-start growth.

The problem? According to collated research and a recent *Harvard Business Review* report, the failure rate for mergers and acquisitions (M&As) sits between 70 percent and 90 percent.[12] I wouldn't take those odds to transform my business.

With the acceleration of new technologies and product development, the declining cost of technology, the world getting smaller (i.e., more closely connected), and the growth in venture capital investment, the disrupter can get disrupted very quickly. It's critical to carve out some time, a person or two, and some investment to search for, validate, and begin working on the next phase of your S curve—or you will undoubtedly face the fate that has claimed the lives of most companies that have come before you.

On the other hand, my excitement and interest comes from building new products and disrupting industries, and I've been guilty of spending too much of my time and too large an investment on creating the new new thing at the expense of managing our current business. I've found that *it takes great discipline to manage the day-to-day conflict of running your current business and looking for and investing in the next big idea.* It's important to note that if you're doing it right, you will be in constant conflict with your leadership team. The simple way of managing the conflict is being disciplined in managing the amount of time and money that you or others spend on the next big idea relative to your current business and sticking to it in good times and bad. If everyone on your leadership team understands the inevitability of the S curve and agrees on the importance and a time frame for coming up with the next big idea, you will be way ahead of the game.

In our case, the change in technology in the 1980s with the roll-out of Microsoft Windows created an opportunity for new competitors to launch with new technology, which gave them an unfair competitive advantage over us. Our only savior for the long period of time it took us to rewrite our software was the stickiness of our product and the large switching costs built in. During that period, we remained the largest player in the market and did not lose customers, but we did not add a lot of new customers, either. Our competitors won the bulk of the new clients.

Attention has to be paid to the S curve, as it is much faster and cheaper to develop technology and new software today, and the switching costs are generally much lower as well. I don't think we would have survived in today's technological environment. The time frames within the S curves have sped up, and being first to market no longer has the clear first mover advantage it once had.

UNDERSTAND WHERE YOU ARE ALONG THE S CURVE

You must always be planning ahead so you have something in the works, ready to launch, ahead of when the S curve levels off. How do you find it? Take inventory of all the strengths that your company has and all that you are building, and think of how you might be able to leverage those strengths to sell additional products to the same customer base; leverage your customer base to provide services to a new customer base, thus diversifying your revenue streams; and listen to your customers. There might be some nuggets of gold in what you can learn from them.

Have your eye on changing technologies; look out for the thing that can most easily disrupt you. This is tough because sometimes a technology comes from left field and disrupts you. So how do you know what's next? Be on the constant lookout:

- Keep a close eye on your quarterly revenue trend, number of new clients added, and any other metrics that are the best indicator of slowing growth.

- Keep your ears out to find out what venture capitalists are backing.

- Attend industry conferences and listen to where they think things are going.

- Speak to customers and ask where they're heading and what their biggest problems are. Ask them about any new, cool company in the industry or anything new and cool that any competitor is doing.

You will never know 100 percent what's next, and you'll have to make a bet. But never sit on sidelines. You have to jump in before there's a sea change and you're not part of it.

The Best Way to Predict the Future Is to Invent It

Henry Ford famously said, "If I had asked people what they wanted, they would have said faster horses." Inventing the future way of thinking led Ford Motor to introduce something entirely new in 1908, the first mass-produced, mass-market automobile, the Model T. But once Ford had customers, he should have listened to them.

In 1920 General Motors, which was a distant second to Ford, hired Alfred Sloan. Sloan's first task was to devise a strategy to crack Ford's lock on the market. He quickly ruled out head-on price competition, concluding that a capital fund the size of the U.S. Treasury would be required to do so. So Sloan determined that GM should not offer cheaper cars, but compete another way: offer better quality cars and a greater variety.[13] By 1923 he gave up on better quality and built a Chevrolet with nine-year-old technology but with a new body of the latest style. This gave the mass-produced car the impression of an expensive luxury car, with a sleek look and more rounded lines. It resonated. With sales surging, Sloan became convinced that to compete with Ford it was not necessary to lead in engineering but merely to offer customers better-looking cars with more choices. GM then developed a paint called Duco, which enabled it to offer cars in multiple colors. Ford's basic black cars were eclipsed by GM's new variety of brightly colored models.

We don't know if Ford was serious when he said "a customer can have a car painted any color he wants as long as it's black" (as discussed in Chapter 2), but if he meant this sincerely, he made a critical and costly error. At that point he should have listened to his customers. GM's sales surpassed that of Ford by 1927. Ford invented the mass-produced car, and his lead in the industry lasted all of 19 years.

I didn't ask my prospective customers if they wanted an OMS. They didn't know they had a problem and therefore didn't know they needed a solution. I delivered the first version, and I had no idea what Merrin Financial would turn into. What I did know is that once you have a customer base, you have a growing source of free ideas on how to make that product or service better. All you have to do is listen to those actually using the products. Not all ideas will be good, but that's where your judgment comes in. If you start to hear the same idea over and over again, that's probably one you should listen to. But if I implemented *every* idea that was followed by "if you do this one thing, everyone will use your product," we would have implemented a huge amount of one-off features and the opportunity cost of not implementing more value-added features would have stunted our competitiveness and creativity. When you have a client base, listen to them and involve them in idea generation and validation and testing beta versions.

A great example of this was our compliance system, which was the idea of one of our clients. Eric LeGoff, who worked for Michael Price, came to me with this idea: "Compliance is a serious headache and no one does it well. We only know we have a serious problem a quarter or two after we violate a compliance regulation. The regulators often find the problem before we do, and then it costs us big money in fines and reputational damage."

It was a little like putting on a seatbelt after you've gone through the windshield. What if we could warn them before there was a violation? I thought this was a gold mine and would be another major advantage of our computer system over the paper tickets; it also offered another reason for customers to buy our products.

Anybody who managed money and had regulatory oversight should have wanted and needed a compliance system. But, of course, like everything we launched, no one wanted our big ideas in the beginning. Nobody had done this before, and once again we had to educate our prospects as to the advantages, and winning customers was very slow going. Our customers were traders and portfolio managers who were not directly responsible for compliance. And compliance departments didn't seem to care.

Again, we had a very strong conviction that this product was a must-have and had huge advantages over the manual process, which clearly did not work. It took five years from when we first offered our compliance system until it became our biggest competitive edge. It eventually became a major reason to implement an OMS, and often it was the product we led with to make the sale.

But it wasn't going to be enough to secure our future.

Our S Curve

You're probably wondering what all this talk about S curves and finding the new new thing has to do with knowing when it's time to sell. The fact is, I wasn't thinking about selling throughout most of the time I was building Merrin Financial. I was always consumed with thinking about what came next.

In fact, I had never even heard of the S curve when I was building Merrin Financial, but I've since come to learn what we went through are fairly normal business problems and technology cycles. Still, it didn't make it any less painful. There's a difference in slopes of the S curve between new product enhancements, features, and even adjacent products that you sell to existing customers and new products that create new revenue streams, address a different set of customers, or create a different business model.

Adding new features and add-on products accelerated the growth in our S curve and probably would have extended the curve further had the technology shift not occurred and stopped us in our tracks. While I knew nothing about the S curve at the time, we were working on our next big thing anyway. We were constantly adding new modules to appeal to and attract more users. We started with U.S.-based equities and then we added international capabilities. We added the compliance module I described earlier, and then got into fixed income. But we needed a bigger idea.

I knew that we could create a whole new competitive advantage and potentially a much larger opportunity if we could extend the order management system to encompass the entire trade cycle by connecting to the brokers who actually executed client trades. It would be Wall Street's first electronic trading network. We called it, appropriately, E-Trade. Unfortunately, we did not register the name so when the online broker E-Trade came on to the scene, we had to change the name to the Intermarket Trading Network (ITN). (Lesson learned: Register everything.)

Even with the OMS in place on our customers' desks, trading was still manual and prone to error once an order was given to brokers to execute. A single order could end up having 50 or more steps involved from order placement through execution and allocation into separate accounts and input into all the systems that require the trade information. Our plan was to go to the relatively few brokerage firms that had enough technology on their side to accept electronic orders and charge the brokers a small fee for access to our network of customers. This would leverage our growing customer base while providing us with a new revenue stream from brokers who were on our network. In order to do this, we had to get a broker-dealer license, convince our existing customers that this was a good thing for them, and get the brokers to agree to pay us to be on the network. The value proposition for our clients was a vastly streamlined workflow with less manual entry and fewer costly errors. The value proposition for the brokers was direct connectivity to our mutual customers and to make it easier for many of their largest customers to do business with those brokers on our network.

This was long before the Internet was available at everyone's fingertips and way before business models were created to take a piece of every transaction done across their platforms, like apps sold in the App Store or music sold on iTunes. We began discussions with the brokers, but their response was extremely negative and they went straight to our clients to protest. While our customers for the most part had endorsed the idea when we talked to them, the level of negative reaction from the brokers turned them against the idea.

This was very bad. It couldn't work without the participation of the brokers and clients. We were forced to abandon our next big thing and what I was convinced would be an even larger opportunity for Merrin Financial. Being in the software industry was never my ultimate goal. The real opportunity on Wall Street was transaction revenue. Facilitating electronic trading would enable us to leverage our current client base and create additional revenue from each new client that came on board. It would be infinitely scalable, widen our margins considerably, and would fuel our growth for years to come. We had invested a lot of time, money, and energy into our transaction network and with the next big opportunity gone, I figured it was time to sell. But like everything else, I had no idea how to do that either. I had to learn on the job.

Just Say No

The enterprise software business is a very difficult business. The transition to Microsoft Windows taxed the company in every way and especially financially—this affected bonuses, which affected our retention, our service and support, quality, and, ultimately, my love of the business.

I was keeping Merrin Financial going, but it was not easy. Our contacts at our largest customer told us they were looking for other systems. Another large customer stopped paying us and quit. The bank pulled our line of credit. My accountant said, "You're essentially bankrupt."

I had to figure out what to do—fast.

> ### TIME TO SELL?
>
> When your future prospects change because something happens in your market and your next growth strategy goes away, you have two choices:
>
> 1. Change the business model as fast as you can.
> 2. Decide it's time to try something else.
>
> When our opportunity to charge a small fee for every transaction we facilitated disappeared, I knew it was time to move on.

I knew that things were terrible, so this wasn't news to me, but it just added to my depressed state. The good news was that we had built a very unique franchise, so much so that various companies were poking around interested in buying a piece of the company. None of them would turn out to be the right partner, but the multiple inquiries validated that we had something of value. We built a business creating the trading infrastructure for many of the largest asset managers in the United States and England. Our systems captured the most valuable piece of information on Wall Street—the order before it has been executed. Most of Wall Street was built around getting access to that order and collecting the commission for executing the order. It was roughly a $15 billion business for equities in the United States alone. While we had competition, we were by far the leaders in the space and had an excellent reputation for innovation, as we created every new product in the space.

But I knew I needed to extricate myself, and what happened next still amazes me. A corporate strategy executive at ADP, a large public company that was the leader in payroll services and had a large and growing financial services division, called and said, "We'd like to come in and talk to you about your business." Since we had gotten these calls before, I suspected it really meant they wanted to come in and talk about buying our business.

We had a very good meeting where I told them about our strategy. Two weeks later they returned and told me how they viewed the industry. It was everything I had told them, now reflected back in their own words. I, of course, thought it was brilliant. They believed we both held the same view for the future; that's why they said they wanted to buy a piece of our company.

I needed an option like this. Desperately. I was dancing behind the scenes. But I played hard to get.

"I'm not interested in selling," I said. "I'm not interested in having a partner."

Although I knew what was happening—and it was not good—from an outside perspective, we looked incredibly successful; we had a roster of major clients, and we were expanding globally. We were the market leader in a fast-growing sector. ADP kept calling.

"Look, I've been getting lots of phone calls from lots of your competitors. I'm not interested in selling a piece and then running it," I said. "If you want it, you're going to have to buy the whole thing or you can buy nothing."

Maybe this sounds risky, but I thought that was what they wanted because they had told me their whole strategy. They had a whole financial division that needed exactly what we had. Buying Merrin Financial would be incredibly synergistic with their business.

We started negotiating for the sale of the whole company. This was my first major negotiation, and again I went to my dad for guidance. We sat for hours role-playing the scenarios. *What is their position?* we asked ourselves. We would think of the different things they could possibly say and write them down and then prepare our responses. Then we would think about how they would respond to our responses. It became a script. It was almost unfair because we had done such a good job prepping and role-playing that the real conversations went exactly as we had practiced. We had anticipated every scenario, every argument and position they would have during the negotiations. This was a stark revelation of how role-playing and being better prepared than your prospects, customers, partners, or potential acquirers can become an unfair competitive advantage. This type of preparation led me to develop the 3×3 negotiating style that is discussed in Chapter 8.

WHAT TO EXPECT WHEN YOU'RE NEGOTIATING

Predicting what would happen in our negotiations wasn't actually that hard. We had spoken to the other side and knew where they were coming from before we started the negotiation. If we put ourselves in their shoes, we had a good educated guess as to what they would say, not verbatim, but the general gist. We knew they would want to get the best price, and there were several tactics to help them achieve that. Some options the other side has in their arsenal to put you in the weaker position include:

- They will tell you about all the issues they will face selling this acquisition to their management.
- They will point out all the problems with the business: competition, size of market, growth rates, financials, and so on.
- They will focus on all the things they will be able to do that you cannot do on your own: management expertise, capital, global reach, larger sales channel, and so on.

Your job, generally, is to get highest price for your product, service, or company, so you have to combat those issues and tactics and do so convincingly.

We went back and forth for months. We agreed that they were going to buy Merrin Financial for $23 million. But it wasn't just about the money. If I were going to continue to run it for a couple of years, I also wanted full autonomy. This seemed to be a bigger issue to win.

I was on a family ski vacation in Colorado, about to leave the house with my kids, when I received a call from the president of ADP. He told me the corporate lawyer took out the autonomy provisions so I should look at the rewritten documents.

"Well, then, the deal's off," I said. "Thank you very much."

I hung up and went out on a ski run, nervous that the whole thing just blew up. What would happen in the long term? Or even the short term? I remember sitting on the chair lift thinking, "We can't afford this vacation!"

A couple of runs later, I got a call on my cell phone from the president of the Financial Markets division at ADP. "The corporate lawyer's on vacation," he said, "but I tracked him down and we put back every word."

The deal was done.

Now what?

WAYS TO APPEAR MOST ATTRACTIVE DURING A NEGOTIATION

- Play hard to get.
- Create competition. Talk about the others in the market approaching you. (We had received a few phone calls by the time ADP contacted us; it was enough to show we had made an impression and people were looking at us.)

- Reiterate all of your strengths, especially any special relationships you have and any unique position no one else has. (In our case, we were still the largest, most innovative company with a very unique franchise of supplying the infrastructure to the largest investment managers who pay the majority of Wall Street's commissions.)

Notes

1. *The Museum of Obsolete Technology* blog; unequivocable.wordpress.com/2012/10/24/sony-walkman/
2. Digital Equipment Corporation (DEC), in *Encyclopædia Britannica* (2015); www.britannica.com/topic/Digital-Equipment-Corporation
3. Ibid.
4. Kyle Orland, "Today's Atari Bankruptcy Latest in a Long History of Corporate Deaths." *Ars Technica,* January 21, 2013; arstechnica.com/gaming/2013/01/todays-atari-bankruptcy-latest-in-a-long-history-of-corporate-deaths/
5. John Davison, "It's Time to Say Goodbye to Atari, Once and For All," January 24, 2013; www.gamespot.com/articles/its-time-to-say-goodbye-to-atari-once-and-for-all/1100-6402808/
6. Ibid.
7. Israel Joffe, "Will Nintendo End Up Like Atari and Sega?" *Fox 5 News,* September 5, 2015; www.fox5ny.com/news/16770535-story
8. Ibid.
9. Ibid.
10. Ibid.
11. Nathan Ensmenger, "Dangerous S-Curves Ahead." *The Computer Boys Take Over* blog; thecomputerboys.com/?p = 676
12. Clayton M. Christensen, Richard Alton, Curtis Rising, and Andrew Waldeck, "The Big Idea: The New M&A Playbook." *Harvard Business Review,* March 2011; hbr.org/2011/03/the-big-idea-the-new-ma-playbook
13. Stephen Meyer, "The Degradation of Work Revisited: Workers and Technology in the American Auto Industry, 1900–2000." Automobile in American Life and Society; www.autolife.umd.umich.edu/Labor/L_Overview/L_Overview4.htm

CHAPTER

5

Business Is a Series of Problems to Solve

Sometimes great ideas can be repeated—and sometimes they can't.

After I sold Merrin Financial, my contract stated that I had to work at ADP, the large corporation that acquired us, for a minimum of two years. To stay true to my entrepreneurial side while I was working for ADP, I bought a software technology that was in the middleware space from a public company and created a company around it called Vie Systems.

Middleware software was all the rage in the late 1980s. It was a technology that enabled the creation of faster data integrations between different software packages and systems. Data integration was a huge issue for every company and consumed a majority of many companies' technology resources and time. We experienced this with every sale we made of our order management system (OMS) platform, so I knew the problem well and had been searching for a solution for the past several years. We came upon this technology and, as we were doing our due diligence, found out that the company was running out of cash.

This technology was right up my alley because it increased efficiency, it solved a huge problem, and the prospect base was virtually unlimited. It enabled nonprogrammers to quickly integrate new software into their existing infrastructure and integrate data more easily into disparate systems. This so-called software "glue" was sold to large companies as a way to significantly reduce the number of resources and time needed for data system integration. Vie had a platform that enabled virtually any company to do this—not just large enterprises. That was a worthwhile proposition, and I knew it offered great promise. This was the right software at the right time.

73

I believed—incorrectly—that this was such a winning proposition that it couldn't go wrong. I wasn't quite ready to start another company; I was busy with my new job (albeit an entirely unfulfilling one), and I didn't have a lot of free time. I therefore decided to put in place the day-to-day management of Vie and took a seat on the board. I tapped former employees of Merrin Financial to run the company, and we waited for the product to sell. The problem? It never sold.

I soon learned one of the most important lessons in business: A great product is not enough. Excellent sales and excellent management are always required.

When it comes to building a business, nothing goes according to plan. When the plan needs to be altered or when you hit a crisis, that's when you define whether you are good at business or not. Business is just a series of problems that have to be solved, and how well you solve them is the determining factor of how good of a businessperson you are. Those who are successful see when they are running straight into a wall—and they swiftly move to avoid it. Maybe they go over it or maybe they go around it, but they surely make some kind of move to ensure they don't smack into it.

We didn't see the wall. We ran right into it.

Our "wall" was how we positioned the product and how we approached selling it. Our approach was, in one word, wrong. It turned out that one of the greatest virtues of middleware—its wide breadth and ability to solve an enormous number of problems—also presented its biggest challenge. The software can be deployed in any company, in any vertical, across a very wide range of problems. That sounds like a lot of greenfield, but in reality it was our albatross. We went into a variety of companies, offering a very broad solution. We expected customers to come up with the specific use and left it to them to identify their problem that could be fixed with our middleware. When you sell something, you have to solve a specific problem—you can't sell a solution to *all* problems.

It took us way too long to recognize this fact. After a year of running into the same wall, we finally decided to stop what Einstein deemed as insanity and decided do something different to achieve the results we expected. We let go of the broad-brush approach and shifted our strategy to sell a much more targeted and industry-specific solution. Geoffrey Moore's book *Crossing the Chasm* provides a detailed solution to this type of problem. He wrote that while you can get early adopters to buy your solution, there is a great chasm that every company must cross to reach mainstream adoption by the majority of its prospects—the pragmatists. The strategy to do that is to focus on a single vertical or industry with a specific solution until you have enough customers, references, and successes to convince others in that industry that your product or service is tried, tested, and ready for prime time adoption. That was the strategy we ultimately adopted.

The first focus was on financial services, a logical place to start as it was an area we all knew well. The plan was to follow the advice in Moore's book and establish a presence in this space and grow references and referrals within this vertical.

With this new strategy we puttered along for another year, but we weren't making a serious dent in the software universe that we wanted. The management team had frittered away a year trying to sell into multiple verticals, and it became more and more clear that it wasn't the right team to lead this company. I recognized that turning it around would cost significant resources and time, and it was not something I was eager to take on.

Once again, just as things were looking pretty bleak, luck came our way and saved us. The founders and original owners of the technology had filed for a patent, which had not yet been granted when we bought it, but was issued right as we were struggling with what to do with the company. This created value in the platform, and all of a sudden our company was worth something to other middleware companies, which led us to an inflection point.

I knew about these windows of opportunity from the sale of Merrin Financial. I had two choices: I could invest more money and change the management team, or I could sell the company. It was an obvious decision.

We fielded several offers, including one from a public database company that had invested in diversifying into middleware solutions. It was a solid deal, my two years with ADP were up, and I was personally ready to move on. I wanted to change the world, and while this was an exciting and difficult challenge, I viewed it more as an investment than a mission that I wanted to dedicate myself to. It was time to look for a new opportunity. We struck the deal while I was on another ski vacation and I signed the papers eager to take on the next mountain.

A GREAT PRODUCT IS NOT ENOUGH

I learned a lot of things from my brief and arm's-length management experience at Vie. I knew there was a need for a product like Vie's and I thought it would be fairly easy to sell it and expand the company.

If we had followed the principles in this book, either we wouldn't have bought the asset if we couldn't figure out how to stack the deck, or we would have begun executing our predetermined strategy the day we acquired the technology and not have wasted a year. We had not figured out our unfair value proposition or our unique selling proposition before we bought the asset, so we hadn't stacked the deck in our favor. At my current company, Liquidnet, we will not invest in a new business or product until we have both.

Don't Invest In Something You Know Nothing About

It wasn't long before something came along that really excited me. It was what I thought was an amazing idea in the health care industry. Through a complicated string of family relations, I was introduced to a medical doctor in Silicon Valley, who was also a great technologist. He had started a software company that aimed to save the lives of intensive care patients through real-time data and data visualization.

Similar to what we did at Merrin Financial, this would take manual processes and computerize them, but this time it would save lives—a truly noble cause and right in my wheelhouse. Anyone who has entered a hospital knows how scary and inefficient the health care system can be. At a trillion dollars per year, it is one of the largest industries in the country and arguably the most inefficient. It shouldn't be too hard to create technology that would bring efficiencies to this enormous problem.

In the late 1990s, patients brought to the intensive care unit (ICU), depending on their condition, were immediately hooked up to a number of machines that monitor and record the patient's vital signs. The problem was that when the nurse recorded the vital signs, the information from the computer was transcribed to a paper chart. Paper charts can't take the data from multiple machines, analyze, or predict what is happening with the patient in real time and, therefore, cannot save lives or improve the health of the patient at the time they are most in need. The information on the patient chart was also vital to many other parts of the hospital, including billing, compliance, reimbursement, inventory, and more, which would all benefit from straight-through processing systems, just as the financial industry had.

The medical software founder occasionally called me for advice about running the company and raising money. I was very impressed with the questions he asked and his worthwhile mission. After six months of these consultations, he asked if I wanted to invest. I was intrigued and inspired: I put in $500,000.

What was I thinking? Sadly, it went something like this, "I know everything there is to know about technology; therefore, let me invest money in an industry I don't really know anything about and it will pay off huge." I'll spare you the suspense and tell you up front, that was a huge mistake.

After six months the founder came back to me and said, "I spent all the money." Alarmingly, he had very little to show for it. I had a decision to make. I could cut my losses and move on or I could double down, fund the technology further, and go to Silicon Valley and run this thing. After all, my previous experience at Vie showed me what happened when I put other people in charge of managing a company. I decided I would go out to Silicon Valley, become CEO, and help the founder run the company.

I thought Silicon Valley was where the big boys played. And now, after the sale of two companies (Merrin Financial and Vie Systems), I thought I was God's gift to software. At this time, I literally thought I could invest in an industry that I knew nothing about and go to a coast where nobody knew me and where I had no connections, and yet I would be very successful.

Furthermore, I was swept up by the cause. What propelled me most was that this idea was something I believed in, something I found meaningful. I was game to bring the principles of technology and efficiency to health care—there was certainly room and reason for it. Because of my success with Merrin Financial, I knew exactly what to do. Rinse and repeat, right? Wrong and wrong. More like a recipe for disaster.

Every month I flew to Silicon Valley and stayed for two weeks. The accommodations weren't glamorous. I lived at the Creekside Inn, a motel right on a stream in Palo Alto. It had a little convenience store in the parking lot. I worked long hours and returned to my room and dined on beef jerky and potato chips for dinner.

Yet I didn't mind because there was so much to love about Silicon Valley. I loved Palo Alto. I loved the sun. I loved Stanford. I loved going south to the beach. I loved the healthy lifestyle— beef jerky and potato chip diet nothwithstanding. I loved meeting people at Il Fornaio for coffee or a meal.

I loved the very casual and congenial atmosphere of Silicon Valley. No one dressed up. People enjoyed being at work; they had fun and were inspired to do their best creative work. It was so different from the atmosphere that defined the offices on the East Coast and on Wall Street.

The level of programming talent in Silicon Valley was jaw dropping. Only there could we hire someone like Jef Raskin, the guy who designed the user interface for the Macintosh. Literally, he was the human-computer interface expert who was credited with designing the look and feel and the user experience of the Macintosh project for Apple in the 1980s. He was also a believer that the health care industry was ripe for improvement, and he had been thinking a lot about how to do it. We gave him our vision of building a system that tied together all the computers on the ICU floor and how we could use it to save lives. He loved the idea and we convinced him to join us. He did incredible work.

With Jef's lead, we built something called the ZUI, the zooming user interface, and it was very cool. You could zoom out and see the entire ICU floor, all the patients, and all their vital signs. You could see flashes going on at the different beds when there was a problem. Then, you could put your finger on the flash and zoom directly into that patient, as far as you wanted to go. It was very fast and very comprehensive, providing a holistic, real-time view of everything going on with every patient. One of the breakthrough features was that the data went across patients so we could tell if there was a trend happening. For example, we could see if patients acquired infections that when detected could be stopped before they became lethal. Other lifesaving features included a real-time check for all medicine being prescribed and delivered for drug-to-drug interactions, another cause of unnecessary deaths in hospitals.

Show Me the Money

But there was something else to contend with when it came to hiring top talent, which I hadn't anticipated. In Silicon Valley, it seemed that everyone was one degree of separation from someone who had gotten very rich from being early at a start-up that made it big. That was the game, the goal, and everyone was gunning to be on that get-rich-quick list. As an employer, it was crucial for me to show the monetization opportunity and the exit strategy. In fact, that seemed to be a prospective employee's primary consideration. As I interviewed developers, I immediately discovered that they knew more about stock options than I did—and I came from Wall Street! They wanted to know what percentage of the company their options represented, and it became clear that if we could not show incredible progress in increasing value within six months, they would move on to their next opportunity. It was difficult to build a company where it felt like everyone was a mercenary.

GIVE PEOPLE EQUITY OWNERSHIP

I didn't like the sole emphasis on financial gain, but it did give me a greater sense of understanding about the importance of ownership—and one that I would take with me to future opportunities. At Merrin Financial there were only three people with equity. At Liquidnet, everyone has equity ownership. Participating in the upside is important.

Being transparent is also imperative. In Silicon Valley, I saw the way company executives were more open with their employees. They shared the financial state of the company with everyone who worked there. Now, at Liquidnet, we share our financial strategy as well as how we are doing against that strategy. This takes place from the very beginning of anyone's time at Liquidnet. We host quarterly State of the Company meetings where we share the good, the bad, and the ugly and invite everyone to ask questions. We want everyone at Liquidnet to be partners in our success, not just employees. The difference? For an employee, it's just a job. For a partner, it's a mission and they are invested in our success. That is why we give everyone in the company equity ownership and treat everyone as partners. That's why we are very transparent in sharing our results and strategies, are open to any and all questions, and remove any hierarchical barriers within the company.

Know When to Pack It In

We had a great mission with our medical technology. We made a product designed to save lives for an industry in severe need of technology and efficiency with a breakthrough interface so simple doctors and nurses could use it without any training. One would think that everyone should have been interested.

But soon I learned another lesson: Incredibly, sometimes a great mission and a lifesaving application is not enough.

We sought to raise money and approached 15 to 20 venture capitalists in the Silicon Valley area. We got in the door, but it then quickly slammed on us. Everyone we met had the same response. They had seen the same problem and opportunity that we did. In fact, they had all put money into tech companies that tried to take on and solve various problems within the health care sector—and they all had lost money. One of the last venture capitalists we saw summed it up rather bluntly, "You are dealing with a very poor and stupid prospect base—there are easier ways to make money."

I'm not sure I'd be that harsh, but the fact was it did feel like we were pushing a boulder up a mountain. We had some initial interest from hospitals, but we couldn't get them to sign a contract. We learned the chief technology officers of hospitals had an average tenure of 18 months. That's very brief—and it made them unwilling or unable to take a chance on a new software platform regardless of how many lives it could save or how much money it could save the hospital. They had the "you never get fired by buying IBM" mentality.

We were running out of money, and without a ready prospect base and rejections from every venture capitalist for primarily the same reason, it became very clear to me that this was not going to work.

This was difficult for all of us, but the founder took it hardest—and lashed out at the rest of us. Every time we were rejected by a venture capitalist or a doctor at a hospital, it pushed him a bit further over the edge. He always felt that someone other than himself was to blame: the developer, the product manager, me. He was the visionary and the domain expert in the space, so I couldn't run the business without him. As he became more erratic, it became very clear I didn't want to run the business with him. I had invested a lot of money and, more importantly, a lot of time away from my family. It was time to pack it in.

HOW DO YOU KNOW WHEN TO WALK? THESE ARE FOUR SURE SIGNS

Unlike the other times when a miracle seemed to come at just the right time, I had no interest in waiting for one. We had no clients and, therefore, no working system or proof of concept—and no chance of selling this business. I was deeply invested—$1.5 million in and 18 weeks spent away from my family. But it was time to listen to the commonality of feedback from the venture capitalists and our prospects, admit the founder was not someone I wanted as a partner, and pack it up and go home. The only turnaround I looked forward to was boarding a plane that took me back to my family on the East Coast.

1. No partner
2. No customers, no prospects
3. No money
4. No validation from prospects and venture capitalists

No confusion. Add those together and the answer is clear: it's time to get out!

You Can Learn a Lot from Failing

Ultimately, we failed hard. But we failed quickly. It all went down in nine months. The other positive is that the experience taught me as much as any of my successes—maybe even more. Going to Silicon Valley was my very best mistake. I'm not just talking about the lessons I learned from failure (you don't actually know everything just because you've done it before), but the lessons I learned in Silicon Valley I brought back with me.

While I couldn't bring the operational principles of the new order management system to health care, I was inspired by the principles of the latest in technology, innovation, and openness that defined Silicon Valley, and I believed those could be applied to Wall Street.

I learned a great deal about technology, including peer-to-peer technology, the next generation of computing architecture that could have incredible advantages over client/server architecture if applied correctly, and the value of focusing on the user experience. At the time, no one on the East Coast was even looking into peer-to-peer architecture or the user experience. In fact, we hired a consulting firm when we started Liquidnet to help us design our platform, and they recommended client/server technology. Peer-to-peer was much better for our new business, and I only knew about it because of my time in Silicon Valley, where people were much more willing to try new technologies and new models. The Bay Area was a few years ahead of the East Coast—and that put me a few years ahead of my competitors when I returned.

My crash course in user interfaces (UIs) and design was also critical to our eventual philosophy at Liquidnet. Through working on the UI with Jef Raskin, who was so integral in the history of personal computers, I learned the value of design. The Macintosh and all its applications shared a common interface, and Jef introduced me to the importance of making everything intuitive and simple. My prior experiences had been with Microsoft, where there was not nearly the attention paid to making the UI intuitive or attractive. The financial world was built around Microsoft products, and the applications were uniformly ugly and difficult to use. It's still the case: the Bloomberg terminal is the most used application in finance, and it's still archaic, with most users typing commands to navigate the system.

What I saw in Silicon Valley later inspired me to bring design to a financial application. When we were developing Liquidnet, our goal was to make the system so simple and intuitive that the instructions had to fit on the back of a business card. We kept that mandate when we released it. If there was a feature that was too complicated to explain, we simply took it out. Our goal was for anyone to be able to sit down and get running on the software within 60 seconds.

I learned another important lesson as well. I had to admit that my forays in angel investing didn't work out well. I realized I was not good at it and I didn't enjoy it. I had to again build something on my own. Instead of investing in others, I needed to invest in myself. It's the only way I've made money. And it's been a lot more fun and definitely more rewarding.

In my new endeavor, I would bring everything I learned over the years and it would operate differently than any company I had been involved with before. Working on both coasts kept me away from my family for two weeks a month, but it also meant that I was home for two weeks not working in an office. During that time, I took my kids to school in the mornings and I picked them up in the afternoons. It was the first time I met their teachers and knew their afterschool programs. I attended their events and ceremonies and I loved it. While at Merrin Financial I was always at work. Now, I knew how much I had missed at home. It never occurred to me how uninvolved I was in my kids' lives and how unbelievably rewarding it was to spend that extra time with them during their formative years. I'm not sure how much it occurs to others who are building their careers, but once I understood what I had missed, I didn't want to miss any more. The importance and priority of family time is something I wanted to encourage in my next business.

I failed in California, but I didn't come back to New York dejected. I returned to the East Coast energized. I brought new ideas with me, and those insights are what led me to my next adventure.

MISTAKES I WON'T REPEAT

- Starting something in an industry I know very little about.
- Working on a coast and an industry where no one knows me.
- Not leveraging previous customers, my credibility and my reputation.

NO ONE'S IMMUNE FROM FAILURE: THREE LEGENDARY ENTREPRENEURS WHO FAILED BEFORE THEY SUCCEEDED

We all read about the victory laps, but even the biggest winners in business had some epically false starts. Here are just three of them:

Walt Disney's first animation company, Laugh-O-Gram Films Studios in Kansas City, had so much trouble making money that Disney reportedly slept in the office and bathed once a week at the train station. The company was done for good when an important distribution partner went bankrupt. But Disney said Mickey Mouse was inspired from his Laugh-O-Gram days where he became "particularly fond of one brown house mouse" that used to fight for pieces of cheese in his wastebasket when he worked alone at night.[1]

Milton Hershey started three different candy-related businesses, all of which struck out. He then found success with the Lancaster Caramel Company. His idea to provide milk chocolate for the masses was the inspiration of the Hershey Company, a subsidiary of Lancaster. Today, it's a stand-alone business and one of the largest chocolate manufacturers in the world.[2]

Bill Gates started Traf-O-Data to process and analyze raw data from traffic counters to create reports for traffic engineers. It was an early entry into the big data explosion that is sweeping the industry today, but this product hardly worked. A few years later Gates and former Traf-O-Data partner Paul Allen created Microsoft. Allen has said that Traf-O-Data was "seminal" in preparing them to make Microsoft's first product because they taught themselves to simulate how microprocessors worked so they could develop software before the machine was built.[3]

Primary Source: Jayson. Demers, "Six Stories of Super Successes Who Overcame Failure." *Entrepreneur,* December 8, 2014; www.entrepreneur.com/article/240492

Notes

1. Kathy Merlock Jackson with Walt Disney, *Walt Disney: Conversations* (Conversations with Comic Artists Series) (Jackson: University of Mississippi Press, 2006), 120.
2. Company information; www.thehersheycompany.com
3. "Interview with Bill Gates and Paul Allen." *Fortune* (via CNN), October 1995.

CHAPTER 6

Develop Your Unique Selling Proposition

After my short stint on the West Coast, I was determined to pursue something big—something transformational. I was also unemployed, which meant I had a lot of free time.

But coming up with my next big idea felt very pressing. It was the late 1990s and I was 39—already old by Silicon Valley standards, where I had just tried to make a go of it. At that time I didn't know most entrepreneurs start their first company in their 40s. At the time, I felt like a failure. Selling Merrin Financial was a big disappointment for me. It was not the huge success I had planned for or envisioned, and it certainly wasn't the payoff I had invested 10 years of my life toward. I knew the truth; I had no choice other than to sell it, and I felt like I had sold out. I was depressed and anxious.

I set up weekly meetings with Eric LeGoff, whom I first met when he was tasked with implementing the order management system (OMS) at Heine Securities and who later joined Merrin Financial. He introduced me to his friend Steve Apkon. Our goal was to brainstorm the next big thing. Steve was renovating the Jacob Burns Film Center in Pleasantville, New York, just north of New York City, and every week we met in one of the desolate offices in the building. Our conversations were all over the place. We had a lot of ideas, but none were very good.

It was more of an exercise. We were flexing our brain muscles, and that work did lead us to ask a lot of questions about what we could do. I had learned some valuable lessons about what *not* to do in Silicon Valley, so I was pretty fixated on going back to where my skill set and experience was and doing something around making the markets more efficient.

At Merrin Financial I knew I had solved a really big problem, but what I didn't know at the time was that it also built the infrastructure needed to solve a much bigger problem.

At this time in the financial world, institutionally managed assets had grown almost 40-fold from the start of the bull market in 1981. That's when the institutional market started. 401(k)s had just been introduced, and there were very few hedge funds. There had previously been very little interest in the market as the annualized return of the Standard & Poor's (S&P) 500 from 1960 to 1981 was only 1.74 percent (including dividends), yielding an entire generation of uninspired returns. From 1981 to 2000 the annualized returns jumped to 11.79 percent. In 1981 the entire institutionally managed sector was only $240 billion. (Today, it's $15 trillion.)

As the assets under management grew, so did the size of their orders. This created some issues. Institutional buyers had nowhere to purchase or sell stock in the quantities they needed to. They had to buy their goods from the retail stores (the exchanges), which were not equipped to handle their quantities. Think about the American Old West and the general store that served the community. That's all the financial industry had—general stores. However, the industry had grown way past the general store. It was as if the industry had all of these new Walmarts, and the only place to source all of Walmart's goods was the general store. It didn't work.

The biggest "Walmart" was Fidelity. It managed over $1 trillion—that alone was four times larger than the entire sector was when I started Merrin Financial. Every time Fidelity wanted to buy and sell stock, it moved the market. No surprise. Much as the general store would not be equipped to sell Walmart 6,000 sweaters, the stock exchange was not able to handle the larger order sizes of the growing institutional sector.

The result was that every time these institutions bought and sold stock, they moved the price significantly against them. If an institution wanted to buy a million shares of something, they most likely had to buy it in increments of about a thousand shares. That's a problem because with every thousand shares, the price moved. The result was that Fidelity, or any large institution, would force the price up, and the more the price moved, the greater the impact was on the returns of all of the individuals who invested their money with that asset manager. That hit wasn't small. In 2001, it was estimated to be over $100 billion a year. It was certainly enough of a problem that, if solved, would be a huge benefit to a lot of people around the world.

Everybody knew about the problem. In fact, a whole industry was created, known as Transaction Cost Analysis, which was built around this problem. It wasn't about solving the problem. The purpose of that industry was only to measure how much these companies moved the stock every time they traded. People paid a lot of money to measure how much they moved the market—not to do anything to solve it. This was my big WTF that inspired my next opportunity. While we would not be the first to try to solve this problem, the industry for the most part just considered this a cost of doing business. But what if there were another way? I asked myself: *How can we create a wholesale market for these institutions? How can we build a critical mass of liquidity in a short enough period of time to keep people's interest and be successful? How can we stop the market moving against these firms and get them a better execution? What are the one, two, or three things that if we solved, we would have an unfair competitive advantage?*

Then, in the middle of the night, while I was away for the weekend in my country house, sleepless and surrounded by the sound of crickets, the solution started to come to me. My biggest entrepreneurial epiphany struck. In an instant I understood how to create a critical mass of institutional liquidity off the exchange—enough liquidity to create an institutional wholesale market. The OMS! It contained everything the institutions wanted to buy and sell. All we had to do was seamlessly integrate into the different OMS systems, convince the asset managers to allow their orders to flow into this new system, and have their liquidity form a new institutional market.

It was simple—so simple, in fact, that I scribbled the mechanics of the idea on a piece of my kids' drawing paper.

The next day, I called Eric LeGoff. "You've got to come into the city," I said.

He came in to meet me, and I didn't say a word. I just showed him the drawing. "Look at this," I said.

"That's it," he replied.

The idea for Liquidnet was born. It was simple. But that didn't mean it would be easy.

HOW DO YOU KNOW?

As soon I thought of the idea that became Liquidnet—named for the network we were creating to solve the liquidity problem—I knew this idea was the big one. How?

1. **It would solve a huge problem.** The idea could solve a global problem in the market, one a massive and growing number of people were concerned about.

2. **There was an educated marketplace.** Different from when I had the idea for Merrin Financial, where no one knew they had a problem, everyone knew this was an issue, and in fact other companies tried to solve it and in the process had invested heavily in market awareness.
3. **It was a huge opportunity.** Every institutional trading entity needed it. We had an opportunity to build a company that could be very large and global.
4. **I was uniquely qualified to deliver the solution.** Since the secret sauce was to seamlessly interface into the OMS I had invented, I was well positioned to solve this problem.

Learn from Others' Failures

Lots of companies had seen this problem and tried to solve it. Morgan Stanley and Fidelity had tried to solve the problem. There was the Arizona Stock Exchange, which wasn't really in Arizona but had received some funding from the state of Arizona. There were others as well, and then there was the granddaddy of them all, Optimark.

Optimark was founded in 1996, three years before I came up with my idea for Liquidnet. It raised $400 million of capital. Every major bank had invested in Optimark because this was going to be *the* solution to the enormous problem with institutional trading. The company was valued at a billion dollars, and that was before it had any revenue. (Can you see where this is going?)

It took Optimark four years to develop its software. It had a huge team (more people prior to launch than Liquidnet has globally today). No cost was spared, and everyone assumed since smart money was invested in this company, it was definitely going to work. There was a lot of hype around the launch, and the company received a massive amount of press.

But the concept was complicated. The Optimark software would ask traders to enter a range of orders and prices (e.g., *At this price I would buy a million shares . . . at this price plus $0.10, I would buy half a million shares . . . at this price, plus $0.10, I would buy 250,000 shares.*) The idea was that having traders put in that range of prices and specifying what they would buy and sell at those prices would enable them to find the best "clearing" price, and they would execute in size.

There were a couple of fundamental flaws in their plan. The first was that that was not how traders traded. Optimark's success was based on building a critical mass of liquidity while changing the way traders trade. Maybe that's possible, but that takes time. What Optimark didn't understand is that you cannot change behavior and build a liquidity pool from zero to critical mass in a short enough period of time to keep people interested.

The result? Optimark had some traders entering these ranges for their orders but not enough to get to a critical mass of liquidity, so even those Optimark enthusiasts couldn't find a match. After a bit of time, if they didn't get an execution on the trade, they stopped trying.

There were other lessons to be learned as well. The system was far too complicated. In order to understand how to use the system, Optimark held a two-day training program called the Optimark Institute. Traders generally have a very short attention span. Traders sat through this two-day seminar, and then almost as soon as they left the class, they forgot everything they learned. By the time the company completed these training classes across the country, the early people who were trained not only forgot everything that they had learned, but many didn't even remember the password to get into the system.

The product was complicated to use. It required traders to change the way they had always traded, and it was not designed to be a seamless part of their everyday workflow. If traders did use it, for the most part it was an annoyance as they did the work but got no executions, no reward. That meant that traders very quickly stopped using the service. Optimark was four years in the making, and it took just one month to fail.

I took everything I learned in Silicon Valley and for the most part aimed to do the opposite of what Optimark had done. The good news was that Optimark had already educated the market extremely well about the problems it was aiming to fix. (We'd seen how hard that was with Merrin Financial.) The bad news was that it was a spectacular failure—it was the dot-com implosion in our industry—and it left a lot of people and firms feeling burned.

A massive number of firms in the industry had invested in Optimark. Many of our future prospects had put their reputations on the line with their technology teams and the heads of their firms because they all had to ante up resources to work with and integrate this new service onto their desks. And it ended in disaster.

Optimark launched its platform a few months before I started pitching Liquidnet and it had already failed. Very few people wanted to hear another pitch to solve the same problem. But I had a new idea with a different solution to the problem—one that I had only because of Merrin Financial. The big breakthrough I was solving for was the same problem that doomed all the previous attempts and in fact all the business-to-business (B2B) marketplaces of the late 1990s: a way to create a critical mass of liquidity on day one.

The OMS already contained everything that firms wished to buy and sell, so all the liquidity that we needed was out there in a system that I had developed. I had the answer to this big problem because I created the OMS. This was the single most important ingredient to building a critical mass of liquidity. If we could design the interface in a way that required minimal to no intervention from the trader, this would be our unique selling proposition (USP). If we could eliminate the information leakage and match size with size, we could eliminate the price movements and provide a unique and much better execution than they could get elsewhere. That would be our unfair competitive advantage and what we would tout to differentiate it and sell it.

Validate Your Idea with "Smart Money"

"Smart money" investors are those whom others respect as savvy investors; they are those who probably wouldn't give you money without doing their homework, although I'm of the opinion that simply following the smart money without doing your own homework is a quick way to lose money. While getting "smart money" investors is certainly no guarantee of success, getting their input and blessing makes the rest of your job a bit easier.

I thought tapping into the OMS was a great solution, and at first look everyone else did, too, but I knew I needed the opinions of other people—people I trusted—besides my family and friends. I learned the value of this when we were trying to raise money for the health care software company. All of the investors we went to had the same concerns. And once you start hearing the same thing over and over again, you have to give it some credence. Learning why others failed and why it didn't work was helpful in deciding what—or what not—to pursue.

Once Eric was on board, we called a few of our smart money industry contacts. We first approached Nathan Gantcher, at that time president of Oppenheimer & Co., who gave me my first job on

Wall Street. We also went to Michael Price, the CEO of Heine Securities, the well-respected money management firm and one of our first customers at Merrin Financial. We then called Larry Zicklin, who was chairman of Neuberger Berman, one of the industry's largest asset management firms.

I had previously sought out Nate, Larry, and Mike for their advice on an earlier idea for a discount institutional brokerage business. There were discount brokers for retail. If it were successful for retail, why not apply that to institutions, I thought. It turns out they were pretty different. I had put together a basic plan and I was excited to present it, but each one of these industry luminaries, separately, tore it apart. "It wouldn't work," they said, and they all gave me very solid reasons why.

They explained that it was the customer of the asset management firm that paid the broker's commission, not the asset management firm itself. Since the cost did not come out of their pocket, they were not as cost sensitive, so they were less concerned about the commission rate. What was more important to the asset manager and what they were more interested in were the services and research they received from brokers. Was there something unique that would give them an edge, which they would gladly pay for with those commissions?

Their critique had sent me back to the drawing board. Now I had a new idea and I wanted their take. I knew they would be honest with me again. This time, we didn't have much of a presentation, just a couple of PowerPoint slides. "We have this idea," I said, when meeting with each individually. "I really need you to tear it apart; that would be most helpful."

No one tore it apart; instead, they said they liked it. Bolstered by their enthusiasm, in each of the meetings I took it a step further. "Okay, I'd like you to be on the board of directors," I said. "And how would you like to give me a million dollars to get it started?"

Nate and Mike agreed right then and there. Larry did not. Larry was a bit more cautious, and as head of Neuberger Berman he had many resources to help validate the idea. To that end, he set me up with the head trader at the investment management firm. Eric and I scheduled a meeting with Larry and the head trader, where I went through the whole proposition. It took probably about forty-five minutes. At the end of the presentation, the head trader said, "I don't see anything wrong with it. I can't poke any holes in it. But I hope to God it doesn't work."

Somehow that was good enough for Larry to commit $1 million. Like Nate and Mike, Larry knew that I had created a business before and had had a successful exit. It also didn't hurt that the market was white hot. Valuations were high. We raised $3 million at a $30 million valuation in January 2000, two months after I had the idea, two part-time people, and a PowerPoint presentation.

SHOULD YOU BE WORRIED SOMEONE CAN STEAL YOUR IDEA?

- Always consider this possibility when approaching people with your idea. I would not approach anyone to validate the idea or for the credibility circle (explained below) if I thought they could do the idea on their own, without me. I didn't approach any VCs who had investments in the space.

- Ask them to sign a nondisclosure agreement (NDA). It can be completely worthless because if someone wants to steal the idea, they can simply repackage it in a different way or say they thought of the idea beforehand. But it does indicate that you are serious about the idea, which may deter them, and it could offer some protection.

Building Credibility Circles

If you want to potentially speed time to market, ensure beta customers, increase your valuation, and overall enhance your chances of success, you want to build circles of credibility. I had a certain amount of credibility at this point in my career, as I had already built a company and transformed an industry. This time, unlike when I started Merrin Financial, people knew me. Now, I also had something else on my side. Smart money—people who themselves had credibility and were well respected and were investing in our venture—that expanded our credibility circle. People more instantly thought, "If those guys liked the idea, there must be something to this."

I wanted to build our credibility circle further. The third circle that I wanted to create was one consisting of the people who would use the service—traders. I called up a bunch of former Merrin Financial customers who were the head traders of large firms. It made sense to start with the biggest companies. They had most of the assets, and if they came on board, everyone else would as well. I called the head trader of Aim Management, which is now part of Invesco, and I also called folks at Putnam and Janus, among others.

I knew that the more expansive your credibility circles, the more you stack the deck in your favor to successfully get financing, a better valuation, beta customers and launch.

Each person that I called had signed up for Optimark. I reached out very soon after Optimark failed, which meant they all had just recently spent a bunch of their own personal chips to get their companies to do all the paperwork, build an interface into Optimark, and get it set up on the desktops. They had expended a lot of resources, there was a lot of hype, and it had failed.

CREDIBILITY CIRCLES PROVIDE A GREAT FOUNDATION BUT DO NOT GUARANTEE SUCCESS

Optimark benefited from credibility circles in the beginning, too. There was a lot of hope for it because many big firms backed it. The credibility that Optimark achieved got everyone to sign up and try it. It also got them an enormous valuation. But while credibility circles can help in raising money, encouraging people to try a service, and getting a high valuation, it cannot guarantee success.

Everyone accepted a meeting with me; however, I'm not sure that anyone was happy about it. Who wants to sit through another attempt to solve this problem where all previous attempts failed and the last one spectacularly blew up?

We prepared for those presentations, and I knew there would not be much time to state our case. We prepared our 30-second pitch. We came in, they feigned happiness to see me, and then we sat down. I knew I had a very short window before they were going to kick me out. But in that short period of time, they started to perk up. They started asking questions, and then they became animated. They saw how this was different.

Once I saw that they got it, I asked them to poke holes in the idea—and they did. The original plan was to have everyone participate in this service—brokers, long-only asset managers, and hedge funds. But these traders were vehemently opposed to that. They wanted only asset managers to be able to access it. They wanted that exclusivity. They didn't trust the sell side, and they didn't want to interact with hedge funds. We agreed to this change.

They also voiced concerns about security. They would be sending their most sensitive information—orders before they were executed into the pool—so how would we safeguard it? We had to assure them their data was much more secure than the way they were trading currently. To prove that, we agreed to retain a third party, one of the big accounting firms, to audit us and make sure all the protections were in place and everything we were saying about their data's security was in fact true.

There were other things they wanted that we couldn't agree to. One of the features that we knew was absolutely critical to our success was our design for automatically "sweeping" all the orders into our pool. This meant that every order in their OMS would automatically flow into our pool without a trader's intervention. This was how we would seamlessly fit into their workflow, our secret for building a critical mass of liquidity and how not to frustrate the traders. We knew the sweep was the critical component to achieve success. The traders would not have to select which orders came to Liquidnet. This was not something that anyone else had asked of them and not something that anyone would agree to without a deep understanding of how the system worked and the protections built in to safeguard their information.

Everyone rejected that feature. A large part of the trader's responsibility was to pick and choose which order to send to which broker and they were extremely reluctant to give that up. It was a control issue, but also one that if we gave up on would destroy the whole model. Orders entered manually would be few, and the number of matches would be far fewer. Traders would stop using the system very quickly. This is what had doomed Optimark and all the other attempts before us. I didn't want to spend time or money on a model I knew would fail. I held firm.

I made it very explicit. "Today, you give a broker an order. That broker then starts calling all of your competitors to tell them that they have this order, and you've just lost all control over where that information goes. Maybe it's a really good broker, and they're being really careful with the information—but maybe not. And the fact is that the probability of finding a cross is extremely small and those calls start the market moving against you."

Then I explained how Liquidnet was different: "In this system, if there's no match, nobody's going to know anything. But if there is a match, there are only two people in the whole world who know that there's something to be done and you're one of them." I also told them that the only way we would be successful and solve the liquidity problem was if they agreed to the sweep.

It was compelling enough to get a few of these guys to agree. At the end of those meetings I asked each to participate on my advisory board. Everyone accepted. This was the master plan. I now had a third circle of credibility. I knew this would help tremendously when we approached other firms and investors. We had the heads of trading at eight large asset managers committed to using the system and helping to make it succeed. More smart money and actual users had vetted the system. Now, investors would know we had something valuable in the works.

HOW DO YOU KNOW WHEN TO ACCEPT FEEDBACK AND WHEN TO TOSS IT?

There are always people who are going to be negative. Most people are constrained by what they know and they can't envision a different reality.

- Don't rely on just one opinion. You have to get enough of a sample set. Approach different types of people. You can split them into three categories, as identified by the technology adoption life-cycle model that describes how ideas spread, which was adapted and extended in Geoffrey Moore's book *Crossing the Chasm* (Harper Business Essentials, 1991):

  - Early adopters (e.g., the people walking around with the Apple watch when it first came out. These people like to be the first one on the block with the new gadget and don't mind the Version 1 bugs and annoyances).

  - Pragmatists (e.g., the people who buy a product after a lot of other people already did and once the bugs were fixed).

  - Laggards (e.g., the folks who are not going to adopt any new solutions anytime soon).

Target one to two people within a variety of prospect firms and elicit their insight. Look for commonality of feedback and prioritize that feedback.

- Have a clear understanding of what's absolutely critical to the success of your idea and don't compromise on those regardless of the feedback.

- Once you've refined the idea, seek to validate it with folks in the industry who have a solid reputation. If they like the idea, they can serve as customers, investors, and references.

Overcoming the No-Go Issues

Things were looking promising with our credibility circles in place, cash in the bank, and large firms as our first potential customers. But we needed to get another stakeholder on board. For Liquidnet to work, we had to interface with the order management systems. I was well aware that the OMS business was a very competitive business. Everyone hated each other, and mostly they all hated me because Merrin Financial was by far the largest, and because I ended up cashing out while they remained duking it out among themselves.

But now I needed them. I had to go to these people—people who basically had pictures of me on their dartboards—and say, "Hey, I'd like you to interface with a new system that I'm building." It wasn't very likely they would be eager to help me. (It was more likely they would be eager to kill the idea.)

Additionally, all of these OMS players as a course of doing business always overcommitted and underdelivered to their paying customers. They didn't have the bandwidth for more and now they were presented with a request do to more work for a new system that had no customers and no revenue.

However, amazingly, the OMS vendors agreed to meet with me. They were cordial, and they ultimately agreed to participate. Not that they didn't try to exact a hefty cost! They asked for 50 percent of the revenue. The business model couldn't support that, but we were able to negotiate that down significantly.

We came to an agreement on the economics, and the two major players "yesed" us along. We now had the missing mission-critical piece in place. We told the customers that everything was ready to go.

Then, when it was time to actually sign the agreement, the vendors suddenly refused. "Sorry, we're not going to do it," they said, offering little explanation. It was a bit too coincidental; it seemed as if the two major OMS vendors that had verbally agreed were in cahoots.

I was totally surprised—blindsided. We had spent six months with both of these vendors kowtowing and kissing rings. Now in the 11th hour they both did an about face and screwed us.

If we couldn't get the OMS system integration, our solution wouldn't work and we were dead on arrival. After a short period of depression and despair, we turned our thoughts to how we could overcome this. Remember that business is just a series of problems that have to be solved. The more creative you are in solving them, the better you are at business.

We needed to get creative. Thankfully, we knew firsthand from being in the OMS business that your priorities were set by your clients. We also knew from our work trying to get early customers at

Liquidnet that there was tremendous pull that could be leveraged from our carefully built advisory board.

We identified and targeted the largest clients of each OMS vendor. If they weren't already on the advisory board, we paid them a visit and invited them to join. They all agreed.

We explained that part of their role on the advisory board was to prioritize this integration with their OMS vendor. It worked. The advisory board members were invested in seeing Liquidnet succeed, and they knew its success rested on interfacing with the OMS. We won over enough large customers of the four biggest OMS vendors that they agreed to prioritize working with us to build the interface. It took longer than we wanted, but we got what we needed—with a little help from our friends.

The $100 Million Question

As soon as we got Larry, Nate, and Mike on the board we asked them to recommend venture capitalists, so we could go raise the money we needed to build the team, build the product, and launch the service. We knew approximately how much it would cost to build this service and the capital-raising market was hot. I also knew that an industry magazine was about to come out with me featured on the cover as one of the top 10 "Innovators of the Decade." It even said, "The industry that he single-handedly created has taken on a life of its own, but knowing Merrin, he'll just go out and create a whole new one."[1] That seemed like a pretty good chip along with our credibility circles to go out and raise money with. We got enough copies so we could bring one to every meeting.

Our board members gave us the names of four venture capitalists, and we scheduled meetings with each. When you meet with venture capitalists, you typically have half an hour to pitch your business. You've got to get the idea across to them quickly. You need to bring your 30-second unique selling proposition. You have to have and share your unfair competitive advantage. If you have both of those, you also have to be prepared for when they ask you, "Okay, what valuation are you looking for here?"

Our prep work taught us that every decent presentation to a venture capitalist usually includes the same graph. In year 5 you hit $50 million of revenue—anything less than that growth curve would not typically be interesting to a venture capitalist. Knowing that they would discount whatever number we gave them and that they'd seen a thousand similar projections, Eric and I sat down and prepared beforehand to go about further differentiating ourselves. We knew the difference in valuation would come from the answer to several questions. How large was the problem and how necessary was the solution? Optimark demonstrated that for us. How large was the opportunity? Market sizing was easy to get—over $30 billion globally. What pieces did we have in place, and how well had we lined them up to succeed? Our domain expertise and our credibility circles answered that. "Okay, so what do you think the valuation should be?" I asked.

Eric tossed out, "If we can get $30 million out of our premoney valuation, that would be pretty amazing."

It would. Remember, it was still Eric, me, and a PowerPoint. I said, "Well, I think we should ask for $100 million."

The market for getting funded was hot, and since I liked my number better, we went with it. That was all the science and math we put into deciding on the valuation. It is important to understand that the timing in the market, the tail end of the dot-com bubble, was a greater factor and had more impact on our valuation than did our business plan.

We had to spend a lot of time prepping for just that question, so we wouldn't crack a smile or lose it right there because if we did, it would be over. We would have lost. We practiced our answer over and over again.

It worked because we targeted a very large global problem with a unique solution; we had my reputation, our smart money board, and the head traders of eight large asset management firms on our advisory board. Three out of the four venture capitalists wanted to give us money. And they all promised us the same things: "Work with us and we're going to help you and your team build this company and help sign up clients."

I pretty much discounted all of that to zero. I told them honestly and point blank, "Thank you, but I'm going to go with the venture capitalist that gives us the highest valuation."

Thomas H. Lee, Putnam Ventures, a joint venture between T. H. Lee, one of the most successful private equity firms, and Putnam, the large asset management firm, had just raised $1 billion for their first venture capital fund. They gave us a $75 million premoney valuation. They put in $10 million for an $85 million postmoney valuation. We were their first investment. The fund wasn't even closed yet when they agreed to invest in us. The lesson in negotiating with venture capitalists and most other people is that if your starting ask is for less, you will agree on some discount to that number. Our valuation negotiation was a great result for two guys with a PowerPoint presentation. We put in place and did all the things laid out in this book, but it was also a sign of the times.

THE MOST OBVIOUS SECRET TO RAISING MONEY: STRIKE WHEN THE IRON IS HOT

We closed our first round of venture funding in March 2000. We played three venture capitalists off each other, and we negotiated down from a $100 million valuation to an $85 million postfunding valuation. The market was so heated that one Silicon Valley investor famously (now infamously) bragged to the press, "The worst we can do is double our money."

On paper, our initial investors almost tripled their money in two months. But if we had waited to raise money only a month or two later after the bubble burst on the dot-com era, I don't think we would have received a $20 million valuation—if we could have raised money at all.

We learned an important lesson, which we repeated later when we issued a bond and raised other rounds of financing: Strike when the iron is hot. Do not wait. In general, the mood of the fundraising market shifts much faster than your business will grow, so frequently the mood of the market will be a large factor in valuing your company. Sometimes this is the difference between life and death and it's always the difference in the percentage of the company you will ultimately own.

The best time to invest is when the market tanks, but most investors don't do that. Instead, people get spooked and pull back. Lots of good ideas don't get funded in times of turmoil, and would-be great companies never see the light of day. Conversely, when markets are white hot, a lot of terrible ideas get funded. Remember Pets.com with its sock puppet mascot who appeared in a 2000 Super Bowl ad, was interviewed by *People* magazine, and made an appearance on *Good Morning America?* In its two-year existence the company lost money on most of its sales and burned through the entire $300 million it raised.

Great businesspeople understand there are times when the markets are open and times when they are closed. They see peaks and valleys and, when possible, they time their financing to peaks.

Make It Super Simple

With enough money to build the product and a sales team to sell it, we were off to the races. We rented some nasty office space (again!) on a dingy floor with a dingy bathroom in a dingy building, with a dog grooming service in the office right next to us. It didn't stink, but it was noisy. Every time we were on the phone there was a dog barking in the background. "What is that?" we were always asked. "Where are you?"

I didn't want the talent we were recruiting to see our grungy office space so we invited them to lunch at a nearby saloon. (The saloon was at one point shut down because of health violations. Seems I could never escape the mice.)

Most of our hiring prospects were ex–Merrin Financial employees. Just about every single person we recruited in Liquidnet's start-up phase came on board. It was like a reunion. But more than that: we were able to accomplish things incredibly quickly because we all knew each other, we knew the business, and we knew better than anyone else in the world how to deliver the secret sauce. Who better to know how to integrate with the OMS than those who built the OMS?

We adhered to the important lesson I learned in Silicon Valley— a mandate to *make it incredibly simple.* This applied to both the idea and the product. We accomplished our goal to make the system so simple that the instruction manual would fit on the back of a business card. It was a single purpose application that would find liquidity without moving the market, without intervention by the trader. It had to fit seamlessly within their existing workflow and be usable "right out of the box." We knew that desktop real estate was valuable and scarce and decided that instead of being a full-screen application like all the others at the time, we would take up only a very little portion of the screen. We designed little "chicklets" that alerted traders to a match and appeared only if there was an opportunity to trade a large block of stock right there and then.

I hired four salespeople: I put them in a room; I gave them a script; and we role-played for days on end. We practiced—everything from a cold call to getting the meeting to having the meeting and, of course, demoing the system. We left nothing to chance. They practiced while walking around the city, standing in front of their mirrors, taping themselves and with their significant others who—to some of their dismay—could do the pitch as well as they could. But by the time we were ready to start selling, the salespeople were ready.

We set a goal: To get to a critical mass of liquidity we needed 100 firms on the system when we launched. As we were developing the system, it became very clear that we were developing faster than we were signing up clients and getting the OMS vendors to integrate with our platform. As the system was getting closer to done, we lowered our expectations to 75 firms live by launch.

Eighteen months after I had the idea in the middle of the night, 14 months after we raised our first venture capital, we had significant money in the bank, a solid team, and a unique product and we were ready for launch. It was showtime. But by the time we flipped the switch and went live, we had only signed and installed 38 firms. It wasn't the 100 firms I wanted, or the 75 I would have settled for, but we made the call that we had to be live and trading to get other firms to commit and come on board. We crossed our fingers and prayed to God for any trades at all.

Notes

1. Ivy Schmerken, "The Top 10 Financial Innovators of the Decade." InformationWeek: Wall Street & Technology, December 7, 1999; www .wallstreetandtech.com/careers/the-top-10-financial-technology-innovators-of-the-decade/d/d-id/1253235?

PART

3

SHAKING UP THE MARKET

CHAPTER

7

Launching a Company Is Both Art and Science

You have a great idea and you think you're ready to go to market. Now what? Congrats, you've just entered into the most exciting time of the process. This is where real-time problem solving comes into play, and you'll soon find that there are tricks of the trade that you can effectively call on—and then there are other events you never could have anticipated.

For us, launching with 38 firms was far fewer than the 75 to 100 we had wanted. But we soon discovered there was a positive aspect, as 38 is a very manageable number, and we needed every one of them to count and trade every match they got. We focused on on-boarding each firm and designing a launch program that would give them a positive and uniform experience and maximize our chances for success. We called it the Navigator Program. We sent an expert—a navigator—into each firm to assist with the launch. We trained these navigators (MBA students we hired) on how to use the system and whom to call if there was a problem. We gave each a cell phone with pre-programmed numbers for support so we could reach and coordinate with everyone. Then, we sent them throughout the country, placing one at each firm, to help with the first three days of trading on our new Liquidnet platform. For all the support the Navigator Program was supposed to provide, it was mostly a marketing tool.

The program worked as hoped. At each firm, a navigator sat in the trading room, answered all the traders' questions, and solved any problems that arose. Most importantly, with the Liquidnet representative present, our new system stayed top of mind. With someone sitting beside a trader, it created excitement on the desk when a match appeared on our system as opposed to confusion, apathy, or fear of the new thing. Excitement led to the desire to trade on this new platform, and we were there to ensure that every match was acted upon and generated as much volume and revenue as we could in the first few days of our launch. There were a few technology glitches, and we encountered some bugs, which we expected and solved pretty quickly.

We had all taken bets on what we expected our first day's volume to be. Some said 10 million, some said 40 million, and others yet predicted 100 million. We ended the first day of trading with 4 million shares. Nobody—NOBODY—had said as little as 4 million shares. It was extremely disappointing.

But, in the scheme of things, 4 million was still a successful launch, and though not close to our Super Bowl bets—which were based on gut-level excitement and enthusiasm, not mathematics—4 million was in line with our business plan. We broke even at 2 million shares, so at 4 million we were profitable on day one of our launch. The 4 million shares also reset our expectations for what to expect going forward: our daily volume would be something greater than zero and less than ridiculous.

We launched on a Wednesday and the plan was for each navigator to stay with a firm for the first three days of trading. I spent the first few days flying to various cities around the country visiting some of our largest clients. The first day of our launch, which I spent in Kansas City, had been frustrating with what I saw as a lackluster amount of shares traded, but what happened next was epic both for the volume we traded and the notoriety we received. I was in Texas, where I was treated like a rock star. I walked into our client's office and everyone was buzzing about Liquidnet.

It was only noon in New York, but I soon learned we had already done 12 million shares. Then the head trader asked me, "Did you see what happened with ITG?" Investment Technology Group (ITG) was our only competitor at the time. They had a different model and had launched 14 years earlier.

"No, I didn't," I said. "I'm just off of the plane."

While I didn't know what happened with ITG, I did know all about ITG. It had pioneered "static crossing," which meant that ITG would pick a point in time, maybe on the hour, and ask clients to put what they wanted to buy and sell into the pool at that time. ITG was trading millions of shares every day. That was because they were the only player in the crossing space. Now, the trader in Texas was explaining to me that he had just seen an analyst on TV telling everyone to sell or short ITG. "Liquidnet is going to put them out of business," the analyst said on camera.

Wow. I couldn't have planted a story like that. I was shocked. And I also didn't think it was possible that we could put anyone out of business in our first week of trading. But now, an analyst I had never met understood that, unlike ITG, Liquidnet offered a real-time continuous crossing platform. And with that, we totally trumped their model. Everyone watching seemed to get it, too. ITG's stock dropped 8 points during the day and closed that day down 5 points, or about 15 percent.[1] Everybody was talking about Liquidnet. There was a huge buzz all up and down Wall Street. A start-up would give anything for that kind of press and certainly opt for that kind of press over revenue any day. It gave us instant credibility that could have taken us years to build.

It was so exciting to be on the client's trading floor and see what was happening with our service. Every time there was a match the computer emitted a splashing sound and everyone ran over to watch. The navigator made sure the trader knew what to do and that the stock was traded. It was so amazing, so seamless; it was magical.

We did 17 million shares on our second day of trading. We were euphoric. On the third day, a Friday, we did 10 million shares. I returned to New York and to a big party that we had only planned on Thursday when we hit 17 million shares. We hosted the event on the upper level of a dive bar where the ceiling was falling down. You should have seen this place! But no one cared; we had drinks and music and lots to celebrate.

We had been working nonstop for the past 14 months in such a whirlwind—people hardly got up from their desk to go to the bathroom. There had been so many ups and downs, it was a constant emotional roller coaster. Nobody had ever created a navigator program; nobody had ever connected all these firms in one place to trade together; all previous attempts had failed, and everyone said "this would never work." Up until this point it was a well-known belief that "there's no way to execute a large block of stock without having a human being in the middle." We proved them all wrong.

Old Habits Are Hard to Break

We came back from the weekend and expected that our volumes would continue to grow. That didn't happen.

While the navigators were there for the launch, it was never the plan for them to stay. First, they were MBA students who had to get back to school. Second, they wouldn't have been allowed to stay on our customers' trading floors. Getting allowances for them for the three-day launch had been a big coup, but approval to stay indefinitely would have been impossible.

Monday came and, unfortunately, without the navigators, we were no longer top of mind. What's more, it seemed like over the weekend the traders forgot everything they learned, and when they returned from the weekend they reverted back to what they had always done, picking up the phone and using the brokers they had always used. However easy it was to trade on Liquidnet, it wasn't as comfortable as doing things just like before. The service was designed to be easy to use—and it was—but it wasn't yet part of the everyday workflow.

This obviously didn't bode well for our ability to execute matches, generate revenue, or create value for the company. We saw a dramatic drop-off in the volume right after the launch. Sometimes we did half a million shares the entire day. We only averaged 3 million shares a day for the first year. In fact, in the very early days, matches became so infrequent that we were given two nicknames: "Illiquidnet" and "LiquidNot."

We weren't losing money. We had been very careful about our expenses, and 3 million shares a day was about breakeven. Still, I couldn't stand it. I didn't understand how it was statistically possible to execute such little volume. Every day I went to our technical people screaming that there must be a bug in the system because there was no way that we could be doing this poorly. I also kicked the salespeople out of the office. I sent them to clients' offices to remind them of our existence and continue to keep us top of mind, reinforce our value propositions, and help them trade electronically rather than pick up the phone, calling a broker and trading manually.

But nothing was going to change significantly overnight. I had to figure out how to dramatically grow our volume because if we didn't, we, too, were destined to have a short life span. Not as short as Optimark's, but we'd ultimately be dead, too.

RINSE AND REPEAT WHAT WORKS

Having the navigators wasn't a long-term tactic, as we couldn't keep the navigators on the trading floors indefinitely. But it became a long-term business strategy for every launch. Every time we opened in a new region, and every time we started a new business, like fixed income, we did so with a navigator program to launch it.

How to Get the First Customers to Sign: Sell in Groups

One thing we found to be most effective when selling a brand new product or service, signing up new firms, or soliciting input or feedback was to hold frequent meetings where we could pull together prospects, traders from different firms, into one group meeting.

Of course, we got some pushback. There were a few firms that didn't want to be in the same room as their competitors, but they were in the minority. Most accepted the opportunity to be with their peers and hear what others had to say and how the others responded to the new offering. What everyone had in common as their largest problem was the serious lack of liquidity.

Traders are generally off the clock by 4:30 P.M., so we planned our meetings at the end of their day. We also had a very good lure. At each meeting we provided appetizers, beer, and wine. It was a great way to get the traders to show up and to talk.

The group meeting was appealing for us for a variety of reasons. First, when selling a new product or service, pitching to a group of prospects at one time can bring together both early adopters and pragmatists so you can sell to both constituents simultaneously.

Both research and firsthand experience show that very few want to be the first to sign up for a new product or service, but if people see others nodding enthusiastically, even fewer want to be the second. In a group setting, where people are engaged, and the product or service seems useful and some attendees are nodding along, the early adopters will want to sign up, and the pragmatists will see firsthand that others are interested—yielding a better chance of signing up both.

Second, when soliciting feedback, if you meet one-on-one with a firm or a trader, you only get the perspective of that trader or firm. In a group setting, however, you can get differing opinions but they feed off each other and ultimately move toward a consensus. Importantly, your customers can hear different opinions and buy into the consensus.

We found that the most effective place to host these group meetings was in the office of an existing customer or prospect. Whether implied or explicit, it was an endorsement—like the hosting firm was giving us a seal of approval. It piques the other firms' interest and desire to participate in the event. In the beginning we ran these group meetings in all the major financial centers. I believe it was part of the secret sauce that helped us sign up the initial 38 firms and certainly the many others that came after the initial launch. It would have been far more difficult and time consuming to do this through one-on-one meetings, and the success rate would have been far lower. Almost always, most of those who attended a group meeting would sign up for our service. Convening in groups became one of our most powerful marketing tools, and we repeated it again and again.

THE SECRETS TO SUCCESSFUL GROUP MEETINGS

- **The most important thing comes down to who's in the room.** Don't mix little guys with big guys. Tackle the big guys first and put them with their peers. If you're a large mutual fund, you don't care that some guy at a small firm is nodding his head, but you do if your large competitor is. That makes an impression.

- **Find the magic number.** A good group meeting requires more than 2 and probably less than 10. You want just enough so that people feel comfortable talking. Five is a good number. There are enough people, but it stays informal and everyone interacts. Be sure to factor in a couple of last-minute cancellations to the size of the group.

- **This is not a lecture.** You don't want stadium seating or anyone in rows. Seat everyone around a table and do not talk at them. You should lead the discussion but let them talk.

Technology—It Gets Better with Age

We were the first institutional broker to execute trades over the Internet. Other brokers had direct phone lines into their customers' trading rooms. That meant that the broker paid for a direct line between the broker and the customer. This was only 2001, and it was the way things had long been done in our industry. We thought that the industry was beholden to very old technology and that the Internet had bypassed the entire institutional brokerage industry. We believed the Internet would have and should have a great impact on the industry.

Initially, clients were concerned about security and the safety of their information. After all, this was their most valuable information being sent over the Internet. We eased their fears by educating them about encryption and the protocols for the messaging software we used and how it was coded in a way that couldn't be hacked. We explained our security measures and precautions in great technical detail, especially to the large companies that were very concerned about security and somewhat resistant to change.

While we got over the security hurdles, we had to get over another, higher hurdle: the Internet itself. We soon discovered—as did our customers—that while direct phone lines rarely went down, the Internet had hiccups, and lots of them. In the beginning every time there was a slight service glitch or a slowdown with an Internet service provider (ISP), our platform would disconnect the users and we had to call every trader and request they log in to the service again. At some points this was occurring five or more times a day. Our five salespeople were spending their days calling our then 70 clients multiple times asking them to log in again. It's probably not a surprise that some said, "I'm done for the day; I'm not logging in again."

Nobody left the service, but they would stop logging in for the day. Some put us in a box and didn't log in for a week or two. That came at a substantial cost. The highest volumes of trading occurred right when the market opened, from 9:30 to 11 A.M., and if we had an outage at that time, the whole day was gone. We'd trade around half a million shares, far less than we needed to break even.

It happened too many times across too many days, over too many weeks. This was all very new to us and as we were the only institutional brokerage firm at the time executing their business solely on the Internet; it was just one of our growing pains. We had to come up with a solution to compensate for the inconsistency of service between the different ISPs. Our solution was relatively simple. Since most interruptions were less than a second, we programmed our software to keep users logged in to our platform and automatically reconnected them behind the scenes. In most cases, the traders never knew there was a disruption. It was a simple solution to an enormously frustrating user experience. Over time, Internet technology improved and became more reliable and more secure so that this issue ultimately resolved itself.

Expect the Unexpected

When we launched, our biggest gating factor to overcome was the concern about the security of our clients' most valuable information. We therefore put very strict measures in place to protect that data, including using numbers instead of firm names and preventing our salespeople from seeing the symbols of the stocks that were matching. We designed it so that when matches were found, only our members could see which stocks were matched. We were so protective of our customers' information, knowing it was their biggest concern, that we hired one of the big accounting firms to independently confirm that their information was protected. We went to great lengths because it mattered so much—to succeed, our members had to trust us much more than they trusted any other broker.

When we talked to our prospects, they told us confidently that they would trade every match we found them so naturally we thought that having the system notify the traders that they had a match would be all they needed to transact in our platform. That turned out to be very wrong. We had to continue to adapt to the realities of the business. In order to keep our system top of mind (post the navigators), we started "nudging" clients when they had a match. Basically, this just meant that one of our salespeople called a client and notified them they had a match in the system.

This practice worked well—so well, in fact, that clients started calling us when they had a match and asking us to nudge the other side. Unfortunately, the human component did not have all the safeguards in place that we had put into the technology platform. One of our salespeople received a call from one of our customers— we call our customers "members"—who told her that there was a match, told her the stock symbol, and asked her to call the other side of the trade. Our platform never revealed the stock symbol, and we had told our membership that the salespeople would not be able to see the stocks that were in the system. She called the other side and said, "I have a match for you in "XYZ" stock. They heard the symbol and freaked out. Though she knew the information from the other side—we were very explicit in telling our members that we did not see any symbols—they didn't believe her. I got on the phone with the member, but they didn't want to hear from me either. They logged out of the system and stopped trading.

They were our largest client at the time—twice as large as our number 2 customer. Losing their business was a massive blow to our revenue and our morale. I had to fire the salesperson; it was not a malicious mistake, but it was the most egregious error possible, and there had to be some accountability. The misstep cost us a tremendous amount of business; it shattered our growth, our confidence, and took us from being profitable back to breaking even.

The client stopped trading for an entire year. They came back because we continued to grow and they were at a disadvantage to their peers who were finding liquidity in our pool. After several years, we were becoming a more important source of liquidity to our members, and we had earned their trust. We decided we would talk to clients and the advisory board to see if they were comfortable with us knowing the stock symbol and they granted us permission. This was a major milestone for us, as it was a very clear indication that we had earned our members' trust and enabled their coverage to make more intelligent calls.

I learned a lesson that would repeat throughout my career: you simply cannot plan for everything. There will be an unknown number of unknowns and you have to expect a certain number of extremely hard knocks. People will take you down a few pegs, or there will be hits to the business through no fault of your own. You won't know where, when, or what it's going to be, just that they will happen. You can't let them derail you. You can be depressed for a bit, but you have to go back to work.

LEADING THROUGH A CRISIS

Okay, so the unexpected just happened. This will truly test your leadership skills. It's time to put on your game face, lead the charge, rally the troops, and figure out how to overcome it. Everyone in the office will be looking at your face, your expressions, your attitude—and that will influence the rest of the people in your company. What matters most now? One word: honesty.

- **Honest communication is the key during the tough times.** Let your people know what happened and what the company is going to do about it. In the absence of communication, people tend to assume the worst.

- **Don't sugarcoat the seriousness of the situation.** Don't give an unrealistic solution or time frame for overcoming it.

- **Use honesty as an empowerment tool.** By being honest with your employees, you'll enlist them in overcoming the problem, which is probably exactly what you will need to do.

- **Don't mope around.** Walk around showing confidence and that will filter throughout the company.

Things You Don't Learn in Business School

On September 11, 2001, we were in a management meeting when someone from member services barged in and said, "I just want you to know that a plane crashed into one of the World Trade Towers."

"Please call our members that work in that tower and make sure everyone is okay," I said. "And please close the door behind you." We all figured it was terrible but an accident. We went back to the meeting, but then, when the second plane hit, we obviously knew something very bad was happening.

From that moment on, everyone in our office huddled around the big TVs. One of the guys who had been with us from the beginning was unable to reach his father, who worked in one of the towers. He was freaking out. Everyone was a mess. Obviously, trading stopped. No one had anything to do but worry.

This is one of those things they do not teach in school or tell you about in a management book. What was I supposed to do? Do I send everyone home? Do I keep them at work? What's the safest place for them? What's the right thing to do?

We all stayed in the office until we gained more clarity. One of our guys who had been in one of the towers during the attack visiting a member walked into the office. He was completely covered in soot. He was in shock, dazed, and traumatized by what he had witnessed.

At that point all transportation into and out of the city had been stopped, and smoke covered the island of Manhattan. We arranged for everyone to get home. Once we knew our employees were safe I started walking home, right in the middle of Seventh Avenue, the only time I've ever seen the streets without cars. F-16s were buzzing overhead. It was completely surreal.

There was a conference held that morning at Windows on the World, the restaurant at the top of the North Trade Center Tower. I had been invited to speak. Generally, I accept those invitations, but this time, I had declined. One person who did speak at the conference was the former head of sales for Merrin Financial. He died that day.

We were all in shock and not thinking much about the business in the months that followed 9/11. Over the next three months, things were slow. Trading all over the world was affected.

We also realized that we, like almost everyone on Wall Street, were utterly unprepared for a disaster. For many financial service firms, 9/11 was a wakeup call that terrorism could happen in the United

States, and we had to think about what to do from a business perspective. Everyone started focusing on business continuity procedures. We had never before thought about what would happen if our building went down or became inaccessible. We were in the world's major financial center and very few firms had disaster recovery or backup plans in place. Like the Y2K-readiness drill that had consumed virtually all companies in every industry the year before the new millennium, business continuity and disaster recovery quickly became a huge and immediate exercise and expense at every financial service firm.

In order to be prepared for this new reality, we had to have a separate physical site from which we could operate in case of a disaster somewhere nearby, but in a different state, with duplicate servers set up with all the applications, connected in real time and backed up. The site had to be ready for immediate use, though the hope was that we would never have to use it. It was an expensive insurance policy. It cost millions—a huge investment for a small firm like ours, which had just launched a little over six months before.

Our first year in business was a struggle. We ran into things we never could have planned for. We didn't reach the volumes we anticipated, and then suddenly there were massive additional expenses and a slowdown in global markets. We had a good product and we were up and running, but we did not have nearly the volume necessary to make us meaningful and important to our customers. We would not be missed if we went out of business. We had to do something big and meaningful because slow growth or no growth meant a slow death. We had to grow and we had to grow fast.

Membership Has Its Privileges

We survived that first year because we had been extremely mindful of our costs, so our breakeven was low. We were actually making a bit of money starting the first quarter after our launch.

We were modestly successful where everyone else had failed because we kept our expenses low, our system was intuitive and fit within our members' existing workflow, and we solved the major problem of creating a critical mass of liquidity in a short enough period of time to keep people's interest. The seamless integration with their order management systems enabled our system to do most of the work for the traders. One elevator pitch was, "Sit back, relax, you don't have to do a thing. We will let you know when we have found you the liquidity you're looking for." We made it all an upside for them and eliminated the frustration of constantly entering orders and getting little in return. With Liquidnet, they didn't enter anything, everything was automatic—they just had a little chicklet on their screen—which would pop up and create a splash noise when we found them a match.

We did grow organically over time as we added more clients and our liquidity pool grew. We relied on early adopters, those people within each firm who liked technology and weren't afraid to try new things. But we weren't growing nearly fast enough to become a meaningful solution to our customer's liquidity problems.

At Merrin Financial we involved customers through our advisory boards. I saw this as a powerful tool, but now we wanted to take it a few steps further. Liquidnet was a unique offering new to Wall Street, and we provided software, technology, and connectivity to an exclusive community. But all the liquidity and exclusivity meant nothing if no one used it. Our members had the problem and in our model they were also the solution. They provided the liquidity, and the more they took advantage of that liquidity and executed the matches, the more actionable and useful our solution would become.

I knew we had to enlist each trader to own the problem and be part of the solution. The more ownership each took in solving their liquidity problem, the better the chance of our success. In essence, we were operating the country club for them, but there had to be some rules to ensure that everyone had a uniformly positive experience. We were the only company on Wall Street that opted to refer to every customer as a "member" from the very beginning, but it made sense. Think about the difference in the level of commitment one feels when you're a customer versus a member of something. As a member, there's a sense of ownership and a greater sense of commitment.

It couldn't just be words, though. We created advisory boards and held roundtables where we solicited their input for member protocols and ideas for new features, and discussed topical issues about our industry. We asked them for their ideas and suggestions. We also asked them to be references for us and to talk to those not yet signed up.

We didn't suggest they do that to be nice to us; we motivated them to take ownership of their success. The platform would be successful only if more firms joined and more traders used it. They understood and they spoke to their friends, their colleagues, and their competitors, mostly unsolicited by us, because they understood it was in their own self-interest to get them into the community and build this liquidity pool. "All of the other ventures failed," they said to other traders, "but here's one that's working." Their feeling of ownership and participation helped fuel the viral nature of our business and it was a huge part of our success—but not all of it.

MAKE USE OF THE NETWORK EFFECT

The Network Effect, popularized by Robert Metcalfe, one of the co-inventors of the ethernet and a cofounder of 3Com, states that the value of a network is proportional to the square of the number of connected users of the system.

In less mathematical terms, this concept explains how a service becomes more valuable when more people use it. Take the telephone. One telephone on its own was useless, and if there were only two, they were not that useful, either. But with many telephones, it became an invaluable way to communicate.

The Internet is another good example of the Network Effect. Initially, there were few users outside of the military and research scientists. But as more lay users gained access to the Internet, there were more web sites to use and more people to communicate with. It grew from there. And individual web sites themselves benefited. eBay became exponentially more valuable by adding new buyers and sellers who joined—and used—the marketplace.

We had the same opportunity. With only a few members on Liquidnet, our value would be marginal at best. We knew the value of our network, our liquidity, and our company would grow exponentially as we grew the number of firms on the network, and ultimately we could change the way trading was done. We explained the laws of the Network Effect to our members and shared data about user behavior. We built a data warehouse, where we examined usage patterns and broke our volume into sectors, industries, and market cap, among many other things. By parsing the information this way, we made it more meaningful to them. It helped them to understand what was executed in the pool the previous day, how they could use it more effectively, and how it was different from other liquidity pools, and it empowered them with the information they needed to get other members on. It had a multiplier effect.

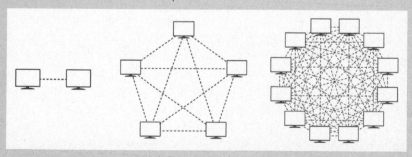

The Network Effect: Two networked computers yield only one possible connection; 5 computers yield 10; 12 yield 66.

Grow Quickly or Die

In the start-up world, slow growth is no different than no growth. It is still death, just slower. We needed a strategy to greatly accelerate our growth. We came up with the idea of setting a metric that required users to commit to trade a certain percentage of matches we found them, which we referred to as the Positive Action Rate. The reason our members signed up was to find liquidity and trade blocks. We were presenting them with more and more matches, but the usage differed dramatically among firms and among traders at the same firms. We had to create a better user experience across our member base, and we had to increase our revenue. What if we set an expectation across the community of at least trying to execute a certain percentage of the matches that the system found them? What would happen if we asked everyone to commit to a 25 percent Positive Action Rate (execute one out of every four matches provided)? We believed, and our advisory board agreed, that if we were going to set that expectation, there had to be some consequence if certain members or traders did not achieve it. The solution was simple: if they couldn't or wouldn't trade 25 percent of the matches, they would be creating more harm than good and we would ask them to leave the community.

We went to the board of directors and elicited their opinion for the idea. They didn't think that highly of it. "Why would your clients care about your threat?" they asked. "It's not as if they're going to miss you. You're only trading 3 million shares a day."

We knew our advisory board, made up of enthusiastic users of our service, felt differently. They were all in favor of it. They knew it would make our pool more actionable, which is what they had signed up for. With that understanding, we had confidence to go to our community of members. We explained, "Look, we created the software and the community, but the benefit of the platform is really based on how often you use it—on how often you take advantage of the liquidity. So, if a member wants to trade and you just sit there, you're not helping improve the trading community, you're hurting it." We told them that in order to make this platform successful, we are asking everyone in the community to commit to try to execute 25 percent of the matches they received with us.

A few said, "Screw you, I'll trade with you when I want and I won't when I don't."

We had about 75 firms signed up at this point and we needed them, but only if they used the service. For the first time we started kicking people off if they couldn't commit to the terms agreed by the advisory board and the vast majority of our members. What happened from there was pretty dramatic. Everyone knew the community needed to be more active to ensure the success of the platform, and those that remained wanted to be good citizens. They took the Positive Action Rate seriously and our volume doubled in three weeks. With those results, the members were happier and so were we.

It worked so well that we very quickly went back to our advisory board and asked if they thought it would be too much to ask the community to trade one out of every two matches. Again, they were really into it.

The result: much happier members and exponential growth. It was the hockey stick growth trajectory we needed. The Positive Action Rate strategy was not in our original business plan, but businesses never go according to plan. New plans and strategies have to be devised in the heat of business as they do in the heat of battle. This strategy was bold and risky and absolutely necessary to our success. We began to hit records every week and then every month. And nobody thought the company could do anything but continue on this path. But, of course, in life and in business, what goes up can certainly come down.

Note

1. finance.yahoo.com/q/hp?s=ITG&a=03&b=10&c=2001&d=03&e=13&f=2001 &g=d

8

Negotiation Skills: Can't Be in Business without Them

In a start-up's early days everyone works tirelessly, but everyone is friendly and happy. Things get rocky at two points: when things go terribly, or when things go really well. As business started taking off at Liquidnet—as revenues started to shoot up—some board members began taking more responsibility for our success. In other words, a few people started getting greedy.

Some of the board members approached me about wanting a larger piece of the pie. Specifically, my piece of the pie. Until that point, our board meetings were very constructive and cordial. As we were ramping up, the directors were patient and reassuring. But now that it was clear the company was going to be successful, they wanted a larger stake. I'm sure they felt they deserved it—and that, with some threats and bullying, I would give it to them. They were wrong. There was nothing in our agreement that entitled them to additional stock. I knew I would never go back on terms of an agreement that we had all agreed to and signed. I would never hand over my equity.

They didn't take it very well to say the least. At one point there were threats to resign.

Retrading of deals happens all the time on Wall Street, but to me the attempt to intimidate me into relinquishing equity in the company I had built was nothing short of blackmail and extortion. If I were less confident of my position or if I had less equity in the company, I could have been forced out. Anyone who reads the financial press knows there's no shortage of stories about CEOs being booted out by activist investors. I was able to stay at the company I founded because I had solid agreements in place, majority control, and 100 percent conviction that I was doing the right thing.

The fact was that these board members really had no basis for their demands. I don't think the board expected me to stand up to them, but that was their mistake. When negotiating, you have to stake out your final position. Once you take that stance, the faster you say no, the faster you will know if you have a deal. In this case my first stand was my final stand. It was hard and there was certainly a downside to holding firm. But the company was clearly starting to take off, and I didn't think they would want to miss out on our success.

This could have been a major distraction, and it could have torn the company apart. We were still in a very vulnerable stage; if news got out that the board resigned, it would have completely undermined our standing. The board members knew that; it was their leverage. But I knew that this one chip would hurt them, too—they were investors, and they would see a positive return only if we succeeded. So, while I couldn't know for sure, I thought they had a lousy hand and that they were bluffing. I played my hand, which I believed was much better.

WHEN TO HOLD THEM AND WHEN TO FOLD THEM

How did I stand up to the board? Two things:

1. **In many respects, negotiations are similar to a game of poker.** You should know as much about your opponents as you can: their motivations, their objectives, their strengths and weaknesses. The more you can understand about what they have in their hand—what levers, emotions, and arguments they will use—the better the outcome will be for you.

   My experience has taught me that most people are very poor negotiators and do not prepare adequately for the really important negotiations. Depending on what the company is ultimately worth, if you give in or if you negotiate poorly, it can cost you from hundreds of thousands to hundreds of millions of dollars. In this particular situation, my conscience made it impossible for me to do anything but say no. This in some sense made it easier for me.

2. **Have your own conviction.** In general, it is important to not only have conviction but to stick to it. Most negotiations are not as straightforward as the one I described and require a greater degree of flexibility, but you always have to have your walk-away position and stick to it. Unfortunately, most start-ups will face a situation where an investor, a vendor, or a customer takes a position that is just so out of line, is so one sided as to be offensive,

and where they have no economic or legal right to be taking that position. In those situations or when you have hit your walk-away position, the faster you say no, the faster you will conclude the negotiations. And in my experience, the vast majority of times, you will get your deal.

There have been many out-of-line, ultimatum-type negotiations in the history of Liquidnet. All of them occurred early on in our development. I've talked about a few of the more serious ones already, but there were more than a few other ridiculous ones, including:

- An industry veteran unilaterally demanded to be on our board and receive stock in the company. If we didn't agree, he was going to make sure we never got started. Sorry.

- There was an order management system (OMS) vendor that had a large customer base outside the United States that told us if we didn't give them 50 percent of our revenue, they were going to make sure we failed in that region. Nope.

- One of the largest investment funds told us when they saw our demo that they should own it and we should operate it for them, and if we didn't agree, they would never come on board. No, thank you!

Choose Your Board Members Wisely

Early on, we enlisted a bigwig from a major bank to help us figure out "clearing," the procedure that would enable us to settle all trades between the transacting parties. This guy was huge in the hedge fund world and a pioneer in the clearing business. We thought he'd be a great board member to advise us on clearing firms, pricing, and other issues critical to back-office functions. He would also be a great asset when we eventually moved to include hedge funds in our member base.

That's what we thought, but that's not what happened. This was a new problem for us. He joined the board, which added prestige, but he didn't do anything that we asked him to do. I was disappointed and surprised by his lack of commitment to the company. While I was a bit concerned about hiring and then firing a board member, everyone was working so hard to start and build this company, I had to expect the same from our board members. Having a less-than-productive employee destroys the morale of everyone who works with that person. I believe the same of board members. I asked him to leave. He was very insulted. I learned that there are a lot of people who want to be on boards for the money, the equity, or the prestige, but they don't want to do the work.

Unfortunately, it wasn't the last mistake I made with board members. Later, we hired another board member who had a very promising track record. The problem was that she agreed with everything I said. That was encouraging at first, and in a way it was nice to have such support, but ultimately, this constant concordance added no value. I needed someone who would challenge me.

Another time, we were trying to extend our reach into Silicon Valley. After an extensive search, we arrived on a great candidate who had been chief financial officer of a prestigious venture capital firm and had many connections into firms in the Valley. He joined us and went through the company orientation before the board meeting. I told him I would be going to Silicon Valley in four months and asked for his help arranging meetings with venture capitalists and private equity companies. As the trip was getting closer—only one month away—nothing had yet been set up. I reminded him that I needed those meetings. By the time of my trip he hadn't set up a single meeting. We parted ways right after.

Everyone has to be accountable to the same rule: if they do not perform, they have to go—as soon as possible.

WHAT TO LOOK FOR IN A BOARD MEMBER

Board members should be chosen based on how they can help your company grow or expand. Each member of the board should check some of the boxes:

- Complement your skill set.
- Have greater knowledge or experience than you in your business or in a business that you will enter in the future.
- Have relationships or connections and be able and willing to introduce you to potential customers or partners.
- Be an expert in legal or regulatory matters if that is critical to your industry.
- Possess specific skills and experiences, such as fundraising, marketing, global expansion, global management, or any other skill that is of great importance to your industry, your business, and your future.

What's expected of a board member should be made very clear during interviews and discussions. In addition to utilizing their expertise and connections, I tell our board members that I expect them to:

- Attend every meeting in person.
- Read all the material sent ahead of time so we can have more productive discussions at the meeting.

- Challenge me and specifically not to agree with everything I say.
- Volunteer to use their knowledge and their relationships to benefit the company.

Becoming Relevant

With the board drama behind us we could focus again on managing the business, which was growing very quickly. We were starting to benefit from just staying in business. We were gaining more members, more word-of-mouth business, executing more transactions—and having more successes.

Think about the first time you went to eBay. You probably didn't buy a car, right? Maybe you found the rare coin you were looking for to round out your collection, an American Girl doll for your daughter, or a pink monkey suit for an upcoming party, but chances are your first foray to eBay was not a big purchase.

The same was true with our Liquidnet members. In the beginning, members were using our platform for decent-size transactions, but they were not as big as they could be and they were not happening as frequently as they could have or, from our perspective, should have.

We saw a huge opportunity to grow with the customers we had. We found it would take anywhere from six months to a year for the traders to be completely comfortable executing on our platform and for Liquidnet to become part of their everyday workflow. But the longer they stayed with us, the more volume they did. Individual usage (the equivalent of same-store sales) went up 20 to 30 percent year over year. It was clear: the longer members were using us, the more volume they did through us. Therefore, we had to do everything in our power to keep them and grow their business with us. With the constant addition of new members and growth in existing member usage, Liquidnet grew 70 percent from year 1 to year 2, 108 percent from year 2 to year 3, and another 108 percent from year 3 to year 4. By the end of year 4, we had over $100 million in revenue and were valued at well over $1 billion.

We believed that once we were averaging 20 million shares a day, we would become meaningful and relevant to the market and an important source of liquidity to our members. We set that target, and once we reached it, we saw that more firms started signing up. It took about four years, but that was the tipping point, and ultimately, with the growth in our daily volumes, we were able to bring the biggest prospects on board. Liquidity begets liquidity and growth begets growth.

Welcome New Members

We were now signing up the largest long-only asset management firms that managed pension funds and mutual funds. We knew however that in order to achieve the next level of growth, we needed to expand our customer base. Many long-only asset management firms had the same view on the stocks they were buying and selling, which meant they bought and sold many of the same stocks at the same time. We always thought opening the platform to certain hedge funds would be the path to adding a lot more liquidity and opportunities for our members to trade and would be the next stage of our growth. Hedge funds were more contrarian than the long-only managers and, therefore, tended to buy when the long-only firms were selling and sell when the long-only firms were buying. The problem was, our members had been certain—and very vocal—about one thing: They didn't want hedge funds included in the Liquidnet pool. Hedge funds in general had acquired a bad reputation and our community was fearful of them, thinking of hedge funds as "smarter money" that would take advantage of the data in the marketplace and use the information against them.

But we knew that not all hedge funds were bad and those members' views were based more on emotion than fact. All hedge funds are not day traders, and many hedge funds had grown large enough to have the same liquidity problems as the long-only funds. Furthermore, an efficient market needs buyers and sellers and a variety of participants. The primary business of mutual fund managers is "long only," meaning they don't short stocks that they think are terrible investments. Hedge funds invest in the stocks of companies they believe will increase in value (going long) and sell the stocks of companies they believe will decline (going short). By playing both sides of the market, hedge funds are generally better "contras" to the long-only managers. And even though hedge funds were a very small percent of institutionally managed assets, they did an outsized share of the trading in the market. The problem we had to solve was how to convince our current members that bringing on certain hedge funds would be beneficial to them.

As always, we went to the advisory board with this issue. We had to convince members that not all hedge funds were bad, and in fact they were able to provide more liquidity. We stressed that hedge funds were an important part of the investment community, and in order to continue to build our liquidity and value to our community, we needed to include them.

It was incumbent upon us to make the argument and to prove to them as best we could why it made sense to open the platform to hedge funds. We had lots of data and we used the data to prove why excluding hedge funds was a bad strategy for the rest of the members. Asset management firms registered with the Securities and Exchange Commission (SEC) have to report their holdings every quarter. While the information wasn't exact, we could tell what was bought and sold by the firms within the quarter by comparing the holdings between quarters. We then broke out the hedge funds from the long-only funds to show the potential matches had those hedge funds been in the community. The data was very compelling.

Once we proved the additional potential liquidity that could be available to them, to further placate their worries we worked with the advisory board to create a list of criteria that hedge funds needed to meet to be included in our community. With the advisory board's thoughts and buy-in, it made convincing everyone else easier. But ultimately we still gave our members control. We offered the ability to opt out or block trading with hedge funds to all of our members. As a further measure, we required all hedge fund members sign an addendum agreeing that they did not engage in a certain kind of trading.

There was a bit of elitism and a lot of concern leading up to the inclusion of hedge funds, but once they were on the platform, it turned out to be drama free: Very few of our members opted out of trading with hedge funds, and the hedge funds exhibited better behavior than many of the long-only funds! Even more important, our theory was right: adding a whole new constituent turbo-charged our volumes.

IT'S ALL ABOUT THE DATA

Data warehouses were an established technology when we launched. Lessons learned from many other industries around the usage patterns of customers fueled the importance to capture the data going through our platform from the very start.

Even before we launched, we went to the reams of established third-party data to point out that our service was designed to help our customers recapture some of the $100 billion in market impact costs incurred due to the inefficiencies in the market structure. That was a very large number that they knew negatively impacted the performance of their funds.

When we started, we couldn't envision all the ways we would come to use the data. But we did know that while retailers like Walmart used data to more effectively manage their inventories, our data had to prove, among other things, that our promise of executing orders in Liquidnet was saving them money and the order execution was better than anywhere else. Over time, some of the other uses became just as important.

- Many of our members often complained that while they were great users of the system, the rest of the community wasn't participating as well. Sometimes they were right, but many times they were very wrong and rather than just agreeing with them, we used the data to prove it.

- Our data continued to be instrumental in our continued marketing efforts and, just as importantly, in the education of the regulators as to the benefit of our unique model on the market structure within each of the countries in which we operated. Examples of information we shared include: the growing number of members in the community, the total percentage of institutional assets managed by our members, our average execution size versus all our competitors and local exchanges, and the cost savings per execution.

When Everyone Hates You

The very idea for Liquidnet was to create a wholesale market for institutions to be able to trade in the large size they needed to execute their orders. Making the institutional market more efficient would increase the returns of all the people who invested their pensions and savings with these asset managers. When we started, it felt like computers and the Internet had completely bypassed the institutional asset management business.

The retail side of investing told a different story. Charles Schwab, E-Trade, and others had put excellent technology and data into the hands of the retail trader. If individuals wanted to trade a stock, they could pull up a tremendous amount of information about that stock, and if they wanted to buy or sell a stock, they could enter and execute that order electronically almost instantly.

But if an institutional trader wanted to buy or sell a block of stock, the only way they could execute it was through a human being. Since there were few to no blocks available on the stock exchanges, the only way to execute a block was to call a trader at a brokerage firm, who would then make calls to other asset management firms to see if they could find a seller.

This was a needle-in-the-haystack exercise that generally ended up having a single-digit probability of finding a match and a very high incidence of information leakage. There are many types of investors and traders in the market, and some of them profit on taking advantage of this information. Knowing that there is a large buyer or seller in the market is the same as knowing there's a supply or demand imbalance. It's Economics 101: If there is more demand than supply, the price goes up. Knowing that, those traders could start buying ahead of that institution and the price would start rising. If no block was found, the broker put the order into an algorithm that sliced the larger order into tiny pieces to get them executed on the exchange—putting more demand pressure on the stock.

To improve on that, we created technology to centralize the block liquidity, solve the supply and demand imbalance by matching size with size, and eliminate the phone calling and information leakage. The result was larger executions at better prices for both parties and the disintermediation of the human sales trader. The result? Increasingly happy members and a lot of unhappy competitors who weren't thrilled about losing their once-essential and highly profitable role.

The way they saw it, our offering would change the balance of power in the industry, ruin their equity business, and threaten their livelihoods. Until that point, the only way an asset manager could access liquidity was through a broker. That had been an incredibly lucrative business model. Furthermore, until we came along, there were two stock exchanges—Nasdaq and the New York Stock Exchange—that executed the majority of all trading. With everyone accessing the same liquidity, there was very little differentiation between the brokers' execution capabilities. A trader could give his or her order to any broker—and he or she could pretty much expect the same execution quality. (Sometimes the larger brokers committed capital to execute their customers' larger orders, which was a differentiating factor, but it was done on only a small percentage of overall orders.)

When Liquidnet came around, since it was for asset management firms only, for the first time the buy-side had access to more liquidity than the brokers did and in a much more efficient model. The near monopolistic access the brokers had to liquidity was broken, and the traditional reasons for using brokers to access liquidity began to fade.

Brokers didn't take this lightly because they risked losing tremendous amounts of money in commissions. Traders at the asset management firms paid billions of dollars a year in commissions to their brokers for what was, for the most part, a highly undifferentiated service, so how did the brokers win their business? Relationships built by providing the services of their firms and bought via dinners, sports events, and more.

The trading desks of mutual funds were supposed to execute orders with whichever brokerage firms offered the best price and service—not the ones that had the best box to the basketball game. However, a lot of business was built around evenings at sports events or steak houses.

Repaying these events became a routine business practice. Having a great night at a game or concert made it easy for a trader to go back the next day and give that broker a large order that could translate to thousands or tens of thousands of dollars in commissions. The trader's job was to execute their orders, and since every broker executed at the same places, there wasn't much difference in execution quality between the firms, so frequently it just came down to relationships.

Like many things Wall Street related, the relationship building got out of hand. The excesses came to a crashing end a few years later when some traders at one of the largest asset managers had a debauched bachelor party in Miami funded by their brokers. Different Wall Street firms supplied private jets, escorts, and some other over-the-top items. It was all reported on the front page of the *Wall Street Journal*. A long-time investigation discovered that taking gifts—such as tickets, cigar-filled humidors, escorts, and drugs—had been happening at some of these firms for years. The firm settled with the SEC for a hefty sum and the industry largely got rid of all that kind of crap.

We did help to change the industry by creating a unique block-only, institutional liquidity pool that provided a very different service from what could be found on the exchanges and a reason beyond relationships to use us. We helped to shift the balance of power from brokers to asset managers by providing access to only asset managers, which put more power and control over the execution into the hands of our members. Execution by way of relationships gave way to execution to achieve the best results for their investors. These changes made me very unpopular among a very large part of Wall Street.

Once when I went to the New York Stock Exchange to do a TV interview with CNBC, our public relations person was in the crowd and overheard a conversation about me. "Who's that guy?" a broker asked another broker pointing my way. "That's the Antichrist," the other answered.

Cultivating Friends

But while one side hated us, the buy-side traders enjoyed their emancipation from the brokers. We wanted to ensure that membership in Liquidnet had its privileges, and we began thinking of ways to deliver that. We started hosting conferences just for our members to meet and talk to their peers. We hosted speakers from inside and outside of the industry and moderated discussions around topics like how the role of the trader would evolve, how that role could become more important as the industry transformed, and how the industry was changing. We focused a lot on their changing role, which was becoming more complicated and necessary as they took more control over their executions. We also framed it the way we saw it, and in a way that they loved. This is the "Golden Age of the buy-side trader," we explained.

It resonated. The buy side, for the most part, had no love lost with the traditional brokers. They knew they had been at the mercy of brokers and had been taken advantage of for a very long time. There were always those traders who had their favorite brokers who gave them the best tickets to the best shows, but for many it had been very much an adversarial relationship.

Many of our members embraced the opportunity to take more control and adopt something that would give them a competitive advantage over the brokers and the other buy-side firms not using us. It created differentiation in the performance of their funds, which made them look smart to the portfolio managers. And it made us win not just their business but their hearts and minds.

As the role of the traders at asset management firms evolved, it became clear to us that there was no training provided by their firms to help them grow into their new roles. The typical training program for a new trader was to sit next to a seasoned trader and do what they did. Portfolio managers, on the other hand, generally had to have qualifications. They had to have an MBA, CFA (a very difficult set of three tests they have to pass to become a Chartered

Financial Analyst), or some other educational background to be hired. We decided that would be a great service we could provide to head traders and created a three-part training program for our members called Headway.

Headway, the brainchild of Jeff Schwartzman, head of our internal learning and development group, Liquidnet University, was not designed to teach traders how to trade. Rather, it was intended to expand their minds about what is possible in their career; how to present their ideas more effectively; how to manage their teams; how to better communicate with their customers, the portfolio managers; and general management training to help them become more important to their firms.

The first part is a three-day intensive program that is half presentation by instructors and half role-play by the participants. The second part is a multiyear coaching and mentoring experience where our instructors coach the participants through real-life scenarios using the tools learned in Part 1. The third part is a two-day intensive course that goes deeper into the skills learned in Part 1 and practiced in Part 2. The classes were sparse at first, as again no one had ever offered this kind of training to them. Even free, we were asking traders to take three days out of their schedule, so this was something we had to do extremely well. We spent a lot of time interviewing traders, getting their ideas, validating and revalidating the topics, and then the instructors spent untold hours rehearsing their parts before we delivered the first class.

We have consistently received rave reviews from everyone that has participated in Headway. Very unexpectedly, I've received e-mails and letters from some of the spouses of the graduates saying that it changed their lives or even helped their marriages. Over the years, Headway has built an international reputation among our community with many traders who received big promotions, attributing the promotion in part to participating in the program. Today, half or more of the participants in the course come from Asia, Australia, and all over Europe.

This program has no explicit return on investment and is a large cost to us to deliver. It is, however, a great example of membership privilege, and by offering a service that helps the careers of our customers, it creates a special relationship with our members that no other broker has. There are, of course, commercial benefits as well: In addition to trading on our platform, our members spend a lot of time with us sharing their ideas or validating ours. When we launch new products, our members tend to give us the benefit of the doubt and try them.

Don't Just Catch Up—Leapfrog

One of the tenets of Liquidnet I'm devoted to is that we live speed. Even before we launched in the United States, we planned our foray overseas. London was calling! It took Goldman Sachs 100 years before they opened their first international office. We did it in one.

If we thought the institutional market in the United States was behind the times, it seemed light-years ahead of Europe. Brokers still took the traders out to lunch and drank pints until they were drunk. A very, *very* old boys network still controlled the industry. Everyone was aware of these factors: we were warned that there was no way that we were going to break into the old boys network.

I didn't heed that warning. I didn't take it seriously, either. One of our strategies was to go global faster than anyone else had. We knew our U.S. members traded European equities, so we came calling with access to a unique liquidity pool in the United States and a good amount of European liquidity. "We come bearing gifts," I said. We believed there had to be enough traders in Europe that would want access to our unique liquidity for us to be successful.

After the first handful of London- and Scotland-based firms signed up, one of them came back to us and said that we could not tell anybody that they were a Liquidnet customer. We wouldn't anyway—we adhered to strict confidentiality clauses—but we asked them why they were coming to us with this now. They told us: "The major brokers have called everyone on the buy side and said, 'if you get on Liquidnet, we will not provide any capital to you; we're going to cut you off.'"

Generally, it's not good business practice to threaten your customers, and it's shocking for vendors to tell their customers what to do, and yet this is a true story. We didn't let it derail us. We stayed focused on our work. We just signed up more clients who were willing to take the risk, and soon there was too much liquidity for others to ignore us. Our success shifted the power away from those bullies and into the hands of our members.

HOW TO UPEND AN INDUSTRY AND GET AWAY WITH IT

Maybe you think Wall Street is ugly, but I think it's like any industry. Anytime there's a disruption, there will be serious winners and serious losers. Generally, the incumbents will never be the disrupters, so they are the ones who will do anything to keep the status quo. Many have made it very personal, even accusing me of taking food out of their family's mouths. Here's how to handle it when the incumbents try to take you down:

- Understand that business is very Darwinian, that what you are doing would not succeed if you were not improving on the incumbent's model, and that if you don't disrupt them, at some point someone else will.

- Don't compete against the incumbents on their playing field. They are established, have existing customer relationships, and are probably much better capitalized than you. You have to differentiate your product or service sufficiently to create an unfair competitive advantage in your favor.

- Stack the deck with credibility circles and make sure you have enough early adopters to get started, who will be vocal and committed to speak on your behalf, to defend you when you are under fire, and to act as references for others.

- Make sure you have enough money or access to enough money to stick around until you get to profitability.

Walk Away

In the four years since going live, Liquidnet was growing incredibly quickly, generating tremendous profits, and was valued at $1.8 billion. We had begun issuing dividends in the second year of operations because we were making so much more money than we could spend. In 2005, we decided rather than go public we would provide a way for our early investors and employees to take some money off the table. We lined up a couple of private equity firms to buy $250 million of shareholders' stock at a $1.8 billion valuation.

Every firm we approached wanted to do the deal. It was too big a deal for one firm, so we chose two, Summit Partners in Boston and Technology Crossover Ventures (TCV) based in Palo Alto.

I wore a purple shirt to the first meeting, which received a lot of comments. I ordinarily wouldn't remember this fact, except everyone from the TCV team came to our second meeting wearing a purple button-down. The point is that if you are a sought-after company, there is a courting period where the firms who want to invest in you will tell you and do just about anything to win your favor. This little detail, I have to admit was very cute and curried some favor.

We came to an agreement on the initial term sheet very quickly, using a negotiation strategy invented at Liquidnet, which we previously mentioned called 3×3. It was based on my experience role-playing with my Dad when I was negotiating the sale of Merrin Financial. It's used when we negotiate any contract, agreement, partnership, or anything else where the desired outcome would be important for our business. It's the planning, prepping, and role-playing that we do in advance, and it greatly increases the odds of a successful outcome. It's called 3×3 because we anticipate three possible responses from our counterpart to our proposal and prepare our best responses to each. We do that for three back-and-forths.

If we do our jobs well, we will have correctly anticipated their arguments and role-played our well-prepared responses to their unrehearsed, on-the-fly responses. We laser focus our responses on getting to the end goal, away from any tangents, minor issues, or argumentative statements that don't move us closer to the end goal. If successful, we will have achieved a successful outcome within the three back-and-forths. And in this case, it worked perfectly. We got what we wanted in terms of valuation and type of security they would be buying.

THE 3×3 NEGOTIATION METHODOLOGY

At Liquidnet we train all of our leaders on 3×3, an easy-to-learn negotiation technique. It works so well that we use it in all significant business negotiations. After learning it, one of our employees came back and told us he started using it at home with his wife. I thought that was unfair, as it always gave him an unfair competitive advantage!

How to do 3×3:

- Determine your opening statement, and then figure out the three ways the prospect can respond.

- Then, come up with the best responses for each of those. Put these three responses down on paper and role-play until you have the best argument for each.

- Figure out the three ways the prospect can respond to each of your three responses, and then come up with the best responses to each of those.

- Then do it one more time.

The goal is not only to correctly anticipate the other side's arguments but to refine your arguments, which will help keep you focused on the desired outcome, limit the number of back-and-forths, and bring you to the ultimate end game. Many times negotiations become bogged down on tangents or non-core issues and then the negotiations end up going around in circles. You want to walk into the room with your well-practiced best arguments and responses and cut off any extraneous discussions or circular arguments.

This is a fairly easy technique to understand, but mastering it requires practice. We have held the equivalent of a debate-off, where we give teams topics and ask them to use the 3×3 to win the debate. We gauge how well they do. Did they correctly judge the other side's positions? We determine if they correctly anticipated their adversary's responses and if they then came up with the most appropriate and best responses. This kind of practice with the leadership team ensures that they not only acquire the technique but also acquire the confidence that it works.

You'll find that using this effectively will enable you to stack the deck in your favor for the really important negotiations. You will be much better prepared than your counterpart. It's an unfair competitive advantage, and it's available for anyone who's willing to put in the extra work.

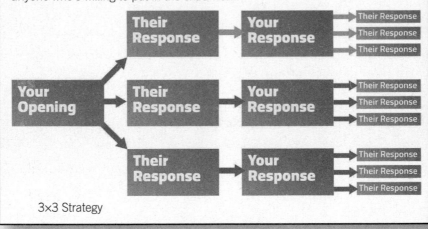

3×3 Strategy

After the main points up for negotiation were agreed upon, then came the brass knuckle negotiations over the finer points. With the price and valuation set, we had to agree on the governance structure and what veto rights on certain operations the private equity firms would have control over. We scheduled a full-day meeting to determine these, and both firms came to the office on the day of Christmas Eve. The TCV folks had flown across the country and sacrificed spending Christmas Eve with their families to get this deal done. There were about 20 of us locked in a conference room for the entire day going over every detail. After we had been at it for most of the day and there were still some major sticking points, I asked the heads of both firms to come into my office with me to see if we could close the deal just between us. We hoped that just between us we would be able to hammer out the rest of the agreement quickly. Two hours later, we could not agree on the final points.

We walked back into the conference room at about 6 P.M. "There's no deal," I said. They had all been sweating it out, waiting for hours for word that we had a deal. You could feel their hearts drop. Their personal commitment and sacrifice to getting this deal done was for naught.

"Let's get some beers," I said.

I told them I enjoyed the process and meeting them, and we hung out drinking beers for a bit before going our separate ways. Of course, I was disappointed. I knew there would be a lot of Liquidnet folks who would be severely bummed out.

But I also thought there was some chance they would come around. We were close enough that I thought it would be silly for them to walk away. I also thought the points of contention were more important to me than to them, so I believed I had to walk away from the table in order to get the deal done.

A few days later, while I was away for the winter vacation, which of course was on the ski slopes, I got a call. Once again, the call disrupting a ski holiday was a good thing. They wanted to move ahead.

It was certainly risky to walk away when we were so close. *In any deal or strategy, you have to hope for the best but plan for the worst.* The terms I held out for turned out to be extremely important to Liquidnet in the coming years. It also helped that the company did not need the money, so this deal was an extremely nice-to-have but not need-to-have deal.

To this day, I believe Summit and TCV came back to the table in part because we were all very gracious and shared some beers at the end. Investors must like your business model, but they are paying for the past and investing in the future of that business, which really means they are investing in the company's management. Ending a very long and contentious day on a nice note showed them something about the ethos of the company and made me someone they felt they wanted to work with. I think we showed our true colors in the face of adversity (we were not bitter or angry), and the fact that there was beer in the fridge endeared them to us.

It Was the Best of Times

We became one of the fastest-growing companies in America. We were number 5 on *Inc.*'s list of the fastest-growing private companies in 2004. We were making so much money that we were able to issue dividends every quarter. Investors couldn't believe how lucky they were to have stumbled into this. Between the dividends and the $250 million of stock that shareholders sold, within eight years of our founding, we had returned $450 million to shareholders on a total investment of $29 million. It seemed we could do no wrong. Our investors and employees had hit the jackpot. I was loving life.

Apparently, so was everyone else. Exactly nine months after we closed the round, an incredible baby boom swept the company. There seemed to be a new birth announcement every day. We had around 30 babies born at that time, which was a large percentage of our workforce. There were so many babies born to Liquidnet employees that two of the babies were given the exact same first and middle names. (In case you're wondering: Maya Rose.) It seemed that we had run out of names for babies.

Some companies—Google, Facebook, Amazon, and Salesforce— seem to keep on growing, but examples of consistent exponential growth are few and far between. They exist only because companies have figured out how to deftly navigate the S curve, determining their next move while they were still far from their peak.

We, too, had to manage our S curve. We knew that our growth and business model would not go unnoticed, and once we had proven that our business model worked, others would copy us. ITG, the firm the analyst predicted we'd put out of business our second day of operation, finally caught on to the advantages of our model and reacted. They had lost significant market share to us, and they understood they had to make some significant changes to compete.

They started reengineering their service over a few years and then launched it to compete with ours. But that wasn't all. The New York Stock Exchange came out with new products, Nasdaq launched two offerings, and virtually every exchange around the world unveiled something they promised would compete with us.

This was new. We'd spent most of our existence disrupting the status quo and educating the markets on our new model to our sole benefit. Now, many others were joining the bandwagon and were competing in our space. What to do?

We took a close look at our business and data and discovered we had opportunities for our members in only 30 percent of the orders traded. That meant that for 70 percent of the orders that we captured, there was nothing we could do for them. They had to go to our competitors to execute the majority of their orders. It was a lot of business to leave on the table. We had to provide new services that expanded our opportunity to execute some percentage of 100 percent of their orders.

ITG, while it lost business to us in the block-trading market, was an early pioneer and had a very large business in all types of electronic execution. We had to add other services and access to all the market's liquidity if we wanted to expand our opportunity across all of our members' orders. It would also solve a somewhat embarrassing problem. While we were the best in the world at electronically executing 1 million shares of a stock, if they had 500 shares left, we only had the ability to execute it manually. To gain the expertise we did not have internally and to speed our time to market, we decided to make our first acquisition. We purchased an algorithmic trading company called Miletus.

It was a smart move, but like every acquisition, there were some issues; it turned out that some of the technology that they were building and we sorely needed was much further from completion than they had represented. We had to hire a lot of developers to supplement their team, which significantly increased the cost of the acquisition and delayed our time to market.

But it worked. We integrated it into Liquidnet and grew it to $70 million in revenue within a couple of years. The acquisition allowed us to expand our opportunity set, sell additional services, deliver a more complete offering to our members, and fuel our growth.

BUYER BEWARE

I think it's fair to say that if a company is for sale, there's a reason it's for sale, and somewhere there is something wrong with it. It still might be a worthwhile acquisition, but it's up to you to find those issues during due diligence. While many will be focused on the synergies and opportunities, there has to be at least one person on the due diligence team who is dedicated to finding the skeletons, issues, half-truths, slight exaggerations, and omissions in the company's presentations and representations.

Every quarter was a record quarter. It seemed like every day we were putting $1 million in the bank. I wasn't surprised at our success—finally achieved. I always believed this was a better mousetrap. And, even at this point, I was certain that we had still only scratched the surface.

But that hubris didn't allow me to see potential issues. All of the success masked a lot of underlying problems. I soon learned that when you have the feeling that nothing can go wrong is exactly when everything can go wrong.

PART 4

DRIVING THE REVOLUTION

CHAPTER 9

No Tree Grows to the Sky

We finally hit our stride. We were constantly breaking new records, and we celebrated all of the successes. When we reached 100 million shares, we rented out a bar and hosted a party. When we hit 120 million shares, we rented out a bar and had a party. It didn't matter that it was only two days later. At some point we could have had a party every other day because we were constantly hitting new records. Everything was great.

Going into 2008 we started preparing for our initial public offering (IPO) at a $4 billion valuation. We didn't need to raise money, but going public had been an implied promise to our shareholders and investors. This included our employees as we gave everyone who worked at Liquidnet equity in the company. The plan was always that we were going to monetize this and share the company's success with the people who built it.

Liquidnet was a super-hot company, and all of the investment banks wanted our business. We hired people to implement all the regulatory and reporting processes required by public companies. We also hired Lise Buyer, who had advised Google on its IPO, to advise us on ours. I don't generally like to hire consultants, but this was an area that required specific expertise. I knew that in many respects the IPO process was deeply flawed and rife with Wall Street conflicts of interest. The bankers would have been through this process hundreds of times, but most of our management team had not done it once. We were woefully outgunned, and we needed help to even the odds to decide who to hire, what questions to ask, and what to ask for; help negotiate the fees; and when to call out the investment bankers if they tried to sell us a bunch of crap.

After an exhaustive process, we selected Goldman Sachs and Credit Suisse to co-lead the IPO, and JP Morgan, Lehman Brothers, and Sandler O'Neill were also involved to help sell the offering. For the first time I was very popular at our rivals, the large investment banks. This became very clear when I got a phone call inviting me to a prestigious conference hosted by JP Morgan in Deer Valley, Utah, in early March 2008. It was super-exclusive—there were maybe 100 people who attended, including the top JP Morgan executives, the heads of the major private equity firms, and industry luminaries like media mogul Rupert Murdoch, oil tycoon and financier T. Boone Pickens, and real estate baron Sam Zell. I was quite surprised to be included in that list and delighted when JP Morgan offered to fly my wife and me out on their corporate jet.

We spent the flight hanging out with the direct reports of JP Morgan's chief Jamie Dimon, including COO Frank Bisignano and Mary Erdoes, head of their global asset management group. Much of the flight was spent discussing the youth village in Rwanda that my wife, Anne, was building to house the orphans of the Rwandan genocide of 1994. It was something completely different, not work related and something that everyone on the plane seemed to be interested in. JP Morgan has a corporate social responsibility (CSR) group that gives millions of dollars to charities every year, and they were very motivated to put their CSR head in touch with Anne. It was a great beginning to an incredible experience.

The conference itself was amazing. It was a beautiful setting, and there was epic skiing and epicurean lunches and dinners, with fireside chats with the biggest captains of industry. JP Morgan was courting me hard. At dinner, Anne and I were assigned to the main table and I was seated right next to Jamie Dimon. That's how important this IPO was to them.

But while it was great fun, there was a heavy weight in the air. As peaceful as Deer Valley was, there was unrest in the world at large. There was talk of credit drying up globally. The head of one of the largest private equity firms had to fly home early because his mortgage securities company was filing for bankruptcy.

I was very concerned. I saw huge red flags portending major issues. I knew a credit crunch of this magnitude could lead not to a recession but to a depression. But I seemed to be in the minority. At the dinner table no one thought much of it. The sentiment was that this was not going to be a recession but just sort of a "blip." I remember Rupert Murdoch said, "This is just temporary."

We all hoped he was right. After a great few days, we left Deer Valley energized and went back to New York—and back to reality.

Call in Connections

About one week after the conference, the economy took a drastic hit when something unimaginable happened. Bear Stearns, the fifth-largest investment bank in the United States, collapsed. It was a warning signal of the financial meltdown that was soon to come. If we were at first unclear as to how we would be affected by the coming financial crisis, it would become clear to us almost immediately.

Bear Stearns was our clearing firm and the largest clearing firm on the street. Liquidnet crossed the stock between our customers, but Bear Stearns did everything else—all of the "plumbing" to get the trades into the correct accounts at the correct banks, and all the funds wired to where they needed to go.

When there were first rumblings that Bear Stearns was going to go out of business, members began calling, concerned that trades done on our platform would not get processed, and some informed us that they had to cease trading on our platform. The volume of calls and number of members discontinuing trading with us increased day by day.

Then, on March 14, the news broke that JP Morgan Chase would acquire Bear Stearns. This was good news, as JP Morgan would continue with Bear's operations and we assumed the news would comfort our skittish members. But it wasn't business as usual.

The world was really going crazy and our members were increasingly jittery about the market. They were particularly unsure about the transition between JP Morgan and Bear Stearns. Those who had stopped trading with us did not come back, and other members were ceasing trading as well. We lost significant volume and revenue. If it continued, we would be out of business due to no fault of our own. We had to figure out a way to remedy the situation—fast.

The JP Morgan conference had afforded me the opportunity to meet—and hang out with—many of the company's top lieutenants. I had a massive long-shot idea, and I picked up the phone and called JP Morgan COO Frank Bisignano. He picked up immediately.

"Frank, I need a huge favor."

"Anything. What can I do?" I explained what was happening. Even though he had inherited the Bear Stearns problem only days before, I said, "I need you to get Jamie (Dimon) to write a letter saying that JP

Morgan is going to stand behind Bear Stearns and back up every trade that we do. And we need it today."

I was completely shocked when Frank replied, "I'm on it. I'll get it done."

Sure enough, by the end of the day we got a letter signed by Jamie Dimon from JP Morgan to our members telling them that they would back up all our trades. We sent it to all of our members. The crisis was averted, and those members who had stopped trading with us came back on.

NEVER UNDERESTIMATE NETWORKING

If this episode with JP Morgan's COO didn't illustrate it, let me tell you that networking is an important part of leadership. If I had not met Frank, he probably would not have answered my call, especially in the midst of the world falling apart. I can't imagine I was his only call that day, so it's a simple matter of human nature to help those you know over those you don't.

- Meeting others in your industry at dinners, breakfasts, conferences, and face-to-face meetings is helpful when you want to do business, need advice or a favor, or—worst case—have to save your company.

- Some people are more comfortable networking than others. If it's not you, then make sure there are folks in your leadership group who can and do excel at this.

- Networking is a two-way street, and chances are that people will want to meet you and ask you for favors. Rather than looking at doing a favor as a nuisance, see it as an opportunity to make a raving fan out of someone. You never know how, where, or when that favor will be returned (if ever), but networking both ways is a numbers game, and over the years you can expect a nice return on the generosity of your time.

The Thing About Market Forces

After filing the IPO at a $4 billion valuation, *Forbes* put me on their list of the 400 richest Americans. I eked in right at the end, number 377, and if the magazine had come out a few days later, I probably wouldn't have made it at all. The issue hit newsstands on September 17, 2008. Two days before the publication date—and two weeks before we were to start our IPO Road Show marketing our company to institutional investors—the world began to unravel and the economic crisis became very real.

On September 15, 2008, Lehman Brothers, the fourth largest investment bank in the United States, and one of our underwriters, filed for bankruptcy protection, the largest bankruptcy filing in U.S. history. The global financial crisis was undeniably here. Every major bank had enormous exposures to each other and so it seemed that every one of the major banks around the world were either in danger of going bankrupt or about to fail. The markets became paralyzed and just about all activity except trading stopped.

Needless to say, it doomed our IPO. We weren't alone; IPO activity in the United States in 2008 dropped to a mere 31 IPOs, down from 213 the year before.[1] They say timing is everything. In this case, it was everything wrong.

Everyone in the company understood that shelving the IPO was due to the market and that it was beyond our control. But everyone was incredibly disappointed. Employees and investors had been counting on a very rewarding liquidity event. The board members who put in their initial capital would have made close to 150 times their money in eight years without the dividends. Our other investors would have made between 20 and 40 times their money in seven years. The folks we brought in in 2005 would have more than doubled their money in two and a half years. Many lives would have changed, and if the past was any indicator of the future, many more babies would have been born.

It was a crazy time, with most of the financial markets at a standstill, banks failing, and the federal government seemingly bailing out another huge institution every week. Many of our members were getting massive redemptions and many others were looking to profit from the panic in the markets and buying stocks of companies that they felt were suddenly very cheap. So while pulling our IPO was disappointing, our trading volumes were going through the roof and we were making more money than ever. Amazingly, 2008—the year of the major market meltdown—was the best year Liquidnet ever had.

It makes sense, of course. As the markets were crashing, many of our members were selling everything that was not nailed down. In our platform we could execute only if there was a buyer and a seller; many of our members were taking the contrarian view and buying during the panic. Those members who bought stocks during the panic ended up having enormous returns over the next couple of years. Another reason our volumes exploded during that period was that everyone was focused on the solvency of the big banks. Our members generally did the majority of their trading with the big banks, but now they were concerned about what would happen to their trades if one of them failed. Little Liquidnet was now viewed as a safer, more solvent company than the major banks in the United States. We did not trade for our own account, take positions, or risk our capital as the banks did, which is what got them into trouble. So our major competitors were sidelined, our members were either running for the hills or running to the fire—but for us, volumes soared and business boomed. To top the year off, I was honored with Ernst & Young's Entrepreneur of the Year regional award.

We entered 2009 wildly optimistic. We went into the first board meeting of the year with strong growth projections. All we had ever experienced in our first seven years was exponential growth. We were confident it would continue, that our tree would grow to the sky. Our board thought otherwise.

Remember the Ripple Effect

In the end, we didn't escape the wrath of the financial crisis—it just adversely affected us much later than it did the rest of the industry.

When the crisis began, investors started pulling their money out of mutual funds. There was a great urgency to sell, and the concern over the solvency of the banks directed a lot of trading our way, which spiked our volume. But, soon—sooner than we had anticipated— clients were done selling and the big banks got bailed out by the government. Our members were left with half the assets they had a few months before, and trading slowed considerably. It was as if the dust settled and everybody—including us—was trying to figure out the new world order and what they should be doing now. We thought the crisis would be limited to the big banks, but we now understood that there had been a delay but the financial crisis was going to hurt us as well.

As 2009 got under way, our volumes were declining and we needed to get a sense of what was going on. We went on a listening tour to gauge the health of our customers. They didn't paint a rosy picture. Visit after visit we found the morale of our members to be abysmal. The stock prices of the asset managers were in the tank. They were engaged in layoffs and downsizings. There were concerns about whether or not they were going to make it out of this alive. The private equity guys saw many of their portfolio companies in crisis, with sales coming to a complete halt.

Up until 2008, all we had experienced—and all our members had experienced—was growth for a very long time. The dot-com crash of 2000–2001 was painful, but it was fairly contained to one sector in the United States. It wasn't a prolonged systemic downturn like we were facing in 2009. The whole world was in a recession at the same time. Investors needed their money and withdrew it from our members. There was no good economic news on the horizon. Our members saw very few investment opportunities, so there was very little trading. The whole world was in a funk with no end in sight. This is what a global financial crisis feels like.

It was a long year. The body blows came fast and frequently. Right after Lehman filed the largest bankruptcy ever, AIG collapsed and required a $180 billion bailout from the government. Whole countries went bankrupt, including Iceland and Ireland, and required international bailouts. The U.S. budget deficit tripled from 2008 to 2009 to fund all the bailouts.[2] Investors began buying tremendous amounts of gold because they felt the government was printing so much money that our currency would become worthless. There were articles and books warning of financial Armageddon and of people building bunkers and stocking them with canned goods to prepare for life afterward. The world was completely in uncharted territory, so the pundits ranged from telling us "The world is coming to an end!" to "Don't panic, all will be fine." The truth is that no one knew, and the uncertainty created paralysis in the business and investment world and that helped fuel the recession.

If the financial crisis weren't enough, the United States was entrenched in and financing two wars. Mother Nature, too, seemed angry. In January 2010 a 7.0 magnitude earthquake and subsequent tsunami hit Haiti, killing more than 200,000 people, and in April 2010 the Eyjafjallajökull volcano in Iceland erupted for the first time in almost 200 years and halted flights across the Atlantic and Europe for five days, creating the highest level of travel disruption since World War II.[3]

Everything was a mess and nobody knew whether we were going to go into a full-blown depression. In January 2009 Liquidnet held a very sobering board meeting. We came with growth projections for the year, and our board cautioned us to reduce our growth forecast and to expect our volumes to decline.

We took their advice, and for the first time we pared back our growth assumptions to flat. That turned out to be too optimistic. Up until then we could do no wrong. Everything we touched turned to gold. But now things were looking more like lead. Our volumes and revenue declined by about 30 percent in 2009.

For the first time we had to lay off people. It was tremendously painful.

This was distressing not only because we were letting people go, which is incredibly hard, but also because we had to admit that we had gotten fat. We had hired a bunch of people in anticipation of going public in order to handle the extra burdens of being a public company, but we had no idea we had gotten so bloated throughout the organization. We had been growing so fast and hiring so many people that when we started really evaluating every person in the company, we found there were a fairly large number of low performers that we probably should have gotten rid of a lot earlier. It didn't make it any easier to lay people off, as we had engendered very much of a family culture, and that, too, was a reason we had let the mediocre players stay on for too long. Ultimately, reducing our staff turned out to be an excellent and very necessary streamlining of our company, reducing layers of management, allowing some of the high-potential younger people to blossom and take on more responsibility, and set us up to manage the company much more efficiently.

That, unfortunately, was just the first round of layoffs—a small percentage of the company—but trading volumes continued to decline, and soon we discovered that the cuts weren't deep enough and we had to reduce staff further. That was excruciating. Laying off people who have lost the fire within, the passion for the company, or were just mediocre is hard but totally justifiable. Laying off great people who did everything they could to help you succeed is agonizing. We made sure that we did it with dignity and with a fair amount of severance. We also helped them with outplacement services, extended COBRA benefits, and provided job counseling. It cost us a lot of money, but we knew that what we did and how we did it in the tough times would be a true test of our culture and character. We knew that, for many, being laid off from the company was no fault of their own and we had to treat them as best as we could.

What to Do When Things Go South

Communicate, communicate, communicate. For the first time we had really bad news to share—and lots of it. Terrible things were happening all over the world. Our employees had tremendous concerns about the economy, our members, our industry, and about how we were going to be affected. *Are we going to be taken down along with the big banks? How are we going to survive? What is our breakeven? How low can volumes go?*

Hiding from these concerns wasn't the answer. We wanted all questions to be addressed as quickly as possible. I knew in bad times we had to overcommunicate. We started holding town halls every month. In these meetings we shared the state of the economy and what was happening with us, with our customers, and with our competitors. I didn't want to ignore the concerns. I wanted to address them, and I wanted all of our employees to hear whatever the news was directly from me.

We were very, very transparent about everything. As the state of the global economy was in a freefall, our outlook could change month to month, and we knew that in the absence of news, our people would probably assume the worst. We communicated much and often. Our people were concerned about layoffs, and many people counted on their bonuses to fund their lifestyles. Bonuses were historically paid out twice a year, so employees were very concerned whether they would continue.

In addition to the truths we wanted to shed light on—even when they were difficult—there were other untruths that spread like wildfire. It seemed that every week there was a new rumor about Liquidnet to contend with. Customers and employees began to come to me with all of the crazy things they heard from brokers, traders, and competitors. Members called me with "news" that *Liquidnet is positioning itself for an imminent sale! The board of directors is going to fire Seth! Bonuses are being canceled! Liquidnet will declare bankruptcy!* One time I was in London and a rumor came out that I had sold all my shares. Most of these rumors were just crazy things, but they all had to be addressed by me personally.

It was as if the sharks started circling. Sometimes rumors can kill a company, but that's only when there's a run on the bank. That wasn't the case here, so all these rumors were simply a distraction. The spread of rumors happens like playing telephone. By the time it reaches back to the originators, it's probably completely different from where it started or much more exaggerated. I don't know who started these rumors or how they started, but there was a period of time where there were so many circulating that we added a "rumors section" to the town halls. I brought them up one by one, and one by one I said, "This is not true."

We took the problems, questions, and rumors head-on. If anybody else heard a rumor, they brought it up right there and then. It was our way of controlling this issue. And that's how we always dealt with the tough stuff—we took everything head-on. You can't shy away from challenges.

TALKING THROUGH TIMES OF TURMOIL

During times of turmoil and uncertainty, you cannot communicate enough. Overcommunicate.

There's a general rule that in the absence of information flowing directly from the company, employees will think the worst. If you're not visible and communicating, employees will either believe that you are oblivious to what is happening or simply that you are not dealing with the problems.

Don't Mortgage the Future for the Present

During this time—despite the difficulties—we continued to focus on two main things. One was not to give up our culture. We had always invested in our people's education, which is generally the first thing that companies cut back on. We still expected all employees to give us their all, and during this time we needed their all more than ever, so we continued to emphasize that in every town hall. We also have a fully stocked snack bar and a fridge filled with soda, juice, and beer, and provide a catered lunch to all employees every Friday. We knew if we cut back on any of that, it would affect the culture and camaraderie, and it would send a clear message to the company that we were in severe distress. The other main thing we did was to continue to invest in the growth of the company. Many companies mistakenly cut this investment in bad times. We continued to invest in new products and in new markets.

But these investments weren't always universally assumed to be right. We were in a constant and contentious debate with the board. We had cut a significant amount of our staff, an amount I believed was as much as was possible without affecting our future opportunities, but the board wanted us to cut more. They wanted us to cut to the bare bone, to stop all investments, and retrench back to our core money-making franchise, the crossing network in the United States and Europe. It might sound counterintuitive that we were able to make these staff cuts and continue to invest in the future. While it was very painful to lay off anyone, we recognized that we had too many layers in the organization. We took some of the savings from the cuts to continue investing in our future growth areas.

The board wanted us to pull back on every area of our business. We had opened operations in five Asia-Pacific countries a few years earlier, and we were losing a lot of money there; it was an enormous drain on our finances. The board said, "Just close down Asia-Pac." They wanted to maximize and preserve whatever cash flow we had, so that we would survive and preserve the remaining value and be able to sell the company if we had to.

I wouldn't do it. Instead of retrenching, I thought there was a case to be made for waiting this out and continuing to build our presence for the long term. And in hindsight, we now know that this was the right call. Asia-Pacific is a profitable and fast-growing market for us now.

The board also wanted us to downsize all of our developments, including the algorithmic business we had entered after we acquired Miletus. No way. That would mean basically giving up all of our growth opportunities. It would have set us back five years. We continued to invest heavily in that business as well.

This was an excruciatingly painful but eye-opening time. I had expected the board to be incredibly helpful and supportive through these hard times. I was looking for the board to be strategic and constructive, to give input, advice, and some encouragement. Every business book I had ever read said if you continue to invest in the downturn, you will accelerate into the inevitable upturn. We were deep in unknown territory with the world economy in the worst recession since the Depression with no signs of light. The board understandably was concerned.

I, on the other hand, was determined to continue to invest in our future growth. We didn't know how long this cycle was going to last. But I knew that I didn't like how the rest of the industry did things. Brokerage firms overhired in good times and overfired in the bad times, so they were constantly getting in and out of businesses in all these cycles. I thought that was a stupid and short-sighted strategy. It was not how to build a good culture of excellent people or a sustainable company. I believed that investing in a downturn is how you leapfrog the competition once the downward cycle is over. The cultures at our larger competitors were solely mercenary. There was loyalty through the next paycheck or bonus and not beyond. It is difficult to sustain a company's culture during tough times, but that is also when it is most important. I believe to this day that we could have gone out of business due to the recklessness of our big bank competitors, but we were able to survive and thrive again because of our strong culture.

The fact was, despite the doom-and-gloom predictions, and because of strategically downsizing operations, we remained profitable every year throughout the entire financial meltdown. The difference was, precrisis, our pretax margins were above 50 percent. We could have maintained those margins had we shut down every new business we were starting, but we made the very conscientious decision to sacrifice our margins to continue building this company for the future.

TO INVEST OR NOT INVEST?

No company is recession-proof. But an interesting 2010 study that examined 4,700 public companies the three years before a recession, during the recession, and three years after found that the ones that weathered the storm shared a common winning formula when it came to deciding how much to pare back and how much to invest.

First, some sobering numbers on the companies examined in the study:

- Seventeen percent didn't make it (they went bankrupt, were acquired, or went private).

- Eighty percent didn't regain their prerecession growth rates for sales and profits three years after a recession.

- Nine percent thrived (they improved on key financial parameters and outperformed rivals in their industry by at least 10 percent in terms of sales and profits growth).

Of the most successful strategies used:

Cutting the most costs isn't the best. Companies that cut costs faster and deeper than rivals had the lowest probability, 21 percent, of besting of the competition postrecession.

Spending the most won't necessarily have the best return. Businesses that invested more than their rivals had only a 26 percent chance of becoming leaders after a downturn. (Scary: companies that were growth leaders at the start of a recession often can't keep up; about 85 percent succumb during bad times.)

Balance is just right. The study found that the postrecession winners "mastered the delicate balance between cutting costs to survive today and investing to grow tomorrow." The ones that deployed "a specific combination of defensive and offensive moves had the highest probability—37

> percent—of breaking away from the pack." Specifically, these companies reduced costs selectively by focusing more on operational efficiency while also investing in the future by spending on marketing, research and development, and new assets.
>
> It's a very tough strategy to pull off to both cut back and continue to invest, but if you do it right, you will focus and invest in the areas of greatest promise, and you will focus on streamlining your organization by cutting the lower performers, layers of management, and improving your operational efficiencies.
> The hardest part is doing it in a vacuum, not knowing when the recession or downturn will end. As long as it is a cyclical downturn and not a secular downturn, meaning the economy is in a downturn and the value of your offering has not diminished, you should take comfort that recessions always end.
>
> *Source:* Ranjay Gulati, Nitin Nohria, and Franz Wohlgezogen, "Roaring Out of Recession." *Harvard Business Review,* March 2010; hbr.org/2010/03/roaring-out-of-recession

The Times They Are A-Changin'

When I saw that the recession was finally coming to an end, I decided to make changes to the board. I thanked them for everything that they had done for the company and the tremendous value they provided during the formative years. Then I asked three of the five original board members to retire. They served on the board for 10 years, were instrumental during our launch and formative years and had made a tremendous return on their investment. It was clear to me that they had provided great value during our start-up phase, but now we needed people who could help us through our next phase and growth into new areas. The hardest thing to do as a manager is to make these types of changes, but as the saying goes, those who got you here are not necessarily the ones who will get you to your future.

Notes

1. *Source:* Renaissance Capital. As cited in Matt Krantz, "Bubble 2.0: Craziest IPO Market Since 2000." *USA Today,* Money, December 18, 2014; americasmarkets. usatoday.com/2014/12/18/bubble-2-0-craziest-ipo-market-since-2000/
2. "Federal Deficit Triples from a Year Ago." Associated Press, October 16, 2009; www.nbcnews.com/id/33348615/ns/politics-more_politics/t/federal-deficit-triples-year-ago/#.V3dLRjkrI_U
3. Clive Oppenheimer, *Eruptions that Shook the World* (Cambridge, England: Cambridge University Press, 2011), front matter.

CHAPTER

10

If You Don't Make Mistakes, You're Not Trying Hard Enough

Liquidnet was now in a unique position—and not an enviable one. We went from everything we touched turning to gold to everything we touched turning to lead. It was a somewhat gradual fall from grace. And it was both extremely painful and very instructive.

Of course, this change from hot to not initially had a lot to do with the weakened economy and the frozen markets. The crisis was a lot worse and lasted a lot longer than anyone expected—and it hurt us much more than we anticipated.

Our revenues declined from our peak in 2008 through the aftermath of the financial crisis, until 2012. We didn't stand still in these years. We continued to invest in new opportunities like algorithmic trading and Asia-Pac. We worked on our systems and our processes; we continued to train our people. But nothing we tried worked. It was incredibly frustrating and demoralizing. As a result, the leadership lost confidence in its own ability to manage out of the crisis, and so did many of the people who worked for us. We had to acknowledge, just as we had previously with the board, that the people who had gotten us to this point were not the right people to lead us out of our problems.

We needed new talent with new skills. We hired people with more management experience who had run or operated larger companies than those of us in Liquidnet's leadership. We needed people who could guide us through this turbulent period, people who could turn the company around and get us back to growth mode. Unfortunately, we exacerbated our problems by making some senior hires that turned out to be less of the right fit than we had thought during the interview process. We had checked their references, which were stellar (who would provide the name of someone who would give a bad reference?)—but the references revealed no clues to the things that turned out to be critical gaps for us.

There have been many books, articles, studies, and metrics on the cost of bad hires. It takes time to find out the hire was a mistake, then it takes time to work with that hire to try to make it work, then it takes time to manage the person out. Throughout that time—depending on how bad that hire is—there is opportunity cost, there is cost of disruption to their department and firm, there are potential morale and disengagement issues of their coworkers, there's loss of respect in the judgment of those who hired them, and there's loss of productivity during training and getting new people up to speed. One estimate says that a poor hiring decision for a candidate earning $100,000 per year could cost, on average, $250,000.[1] No firm can afford to make many of those mistakes. The lesson here is that with senior hires, you need to make tough decisions quickly. And we were forced to make these tough choices.

It's All About the People

Growth can mask many cracks in a foundation, but when growth stops or reverses, those cracks become very evident very quickly. The world had experienced a financial meltdown, and our revenues were declining in the aftermath.

U.S. revenue accounted for 80 percent of our global revenue, and none of the strategies we employed to reverse the revenue slide were working. I met with the finance folks responsible for this profit-and-loss statement (P&L) to get weekly updates. It soon became clear that the numbers were not lining up with what I was being told from the people in charge of the U.S. business. I didn't feel like I was getting the straight facts. I started asking more questions and speaking with our sales team directly. Their answers furthered my suspicions. As I looked for information elsewhere in the organization, I soon found there was a serious disconnect between what I was learning from those at the top and what I was hearing from sales-people on the ground.

This example shows a key problem. You need to get consistent information from those at the top and those working with the clients day-to-day. I needed to correct this issue fast. This is another example of how tough decisions need to be made quickly. We needed to make a personnel change and we did. Another common problem is when a big revenue producer or business lead lacks the management skills you want for your leaders. We had a head of an extremely profitable region not exhibiting the right leadership skills. He was coming in conflict with his own people and leaders across the organization. As mentioned elsewhere in this book, at Liquidnet, culture is paramount, and the culture this was creating was not what we wanted. We had to make a difficult decision to part ways, despite the region doing well financially. Profitability cannot justify tolerating undue conflict or not staying true to your company's core values.

One important lesson we learned as a result of these situations is that we did not have a logical successor in place to either of these roles—someone who we had identified, groomed, trained, and was experienced enough if and when it was necessary. It is an oversight that far too many organizations make yet one that is completely avoidable.

WHO'S NEXT IN LINE?

Succession planning is something that every organization should be prepared for and not just at the top of the organization. Every person in leadership should have a designated successor or even a few that they are actively training, giving more responsibility to, and putting into new situations to gain more diverse experiences.

General Electric has long prided itself in its human resource functions. Jack Welch, who ran General Electric from 1981 to 2001, increased revenue from $27 billion to $130 billion. The market value of the company rose from $14 billion to $410 billion, making it the most valuable company on earth for a while. He was the first CEO at a major corporation to have the Human Resource function report to the CEO and raised the level of HR from a benefits function to a strategic corporate function. Training and succession were among the most important functions within GE, and HR presided over them. Succession planning is so ingrained in its corporate culture that it would be unthinkable for GE to hire from outside for a senior position.

This is in stark contrast to companies like Citigroup, Boeing, Ford Motor, Hewlett-Packard, JCPenney, among many others. They could not find a successor among the tens of thousands of employees already working for them and had to recruit a CEO from outside the company.

You Can't Have It All

As revenues continued to decline, there was no visibility as to when the recession would end. It became clear that we were investing in too many projects that were draining money and we had to make difficult decisions. I have always said that I am not happy unless we are losing money somewhere. By this I mean that I constantly want to invest in new ideas, projects, and/or businesses. When our tree was growing to the sky, we could afford to invest in many projects at the same time. But when revenue is declining and you have to lay off people—you simply can't do everything.

In our case, we had started building a program trading platform we called Liquidnet 4.0. This platform was designed to address a whole new customer segment within our existing customers, whose business was complimentary to our existing business.

Liquidnet began with a single-purpose application. It was a very small footprint that did one thing—it found liquidity and allowed our members to trade in large quantities. Finding institutional size liquidity solved the number one problem for asset managers, and the Liquidnet app did it better than any other human being or application in the world. We asked our members to place all their orders into the Liquidnet pool, and when there was a match, the app would inform them that there was an opportunity to trade in size. On average, we were able to match around 15 percent of the shares in our pool. We had gained a very valuable place on the trader's desktop and those asset managers put billions of shares of orders every day into our pool. But for 85 percent of those shares, we had to tell our members to go elsewhere to execute them.

Our vision is to make markets more efficient, and our first milestone was to be best in the world at trading blocks. We were building unique institutional liquidity pools in every country in which we traded, and ultimately we had to provide our members the ability to execute all their orders any way they wanted. Now that we were a global broker, we had to expand our capabilities to become a full service broker and create an opportunity to execute the 85 percent of our member's shares that we were turning away every day. We knew we could be the best in the world at executing any of our member's orders if we could access both our own liquidity pool and the liquidity in the market available to every other brokerage firm. Execution quality is only as good as the liquidity one can access. With the unique liquidity in our pool we would have access to much more liquidity than our competitors, thus giving us a competitive advantage.

With the acquisition of Miletus in 2007, we brought on a group of very smart people who had built a very complementary business to ours. They had technology, expertise, and access to the rest of the market's liquidity, all of which we lacked and all of which we needed to build out the next phase of our business. Liquidnet 4.0 provided a path to pull everything together, offer members the ability to execute all their orders, and grow our business with them.

We were still losing a considerable amount of money in Asia-Pacific. Our global strategy was important to our future goals, and we knew if we pulled out of the region, it would be twice as hard and twice as expensive to get back in. So we continued to invest in that region. We remained profitable in our other regions and overall as a company but our revenue and profits were declining just about every quarter. One of the people on our leadership team summed it up as constantly going up the down escalator.

We had been working on Liquidnet 4.0 for about two years. We talked about it all the time with great excitement and hope during this period. When just about all the news was bad in our monthly town hall meetings, I would point to Liquidnet 4.0 as an example of where we continued to invest and as a project that represented our bright future. It was a high-profile project, and I touted it hard.

Unfortunately, when we delivered the beta version to our beta customers, it became very clear we had badly missed the mark. What we needed was an updated application that was more extensible and scalable and provided a platform from which we could launch new revenue opportunities for Liquidnet. It had to accomplish all of that while being seen as just an upgrade for our members. Instead, Liquidnet 4.0 had a lot of missing pieces from our existing functionality and was heavily focused on program trading, which would have opened up new business opportunities but solved problems for only a small percentage of our current members. We could not provide it as an upgrade to our current platform because it was so different from the existing platform with additional functionality that most of our members didn't need.

WHAT WENT WRONG . . .

The development of our version 4.0 platform went disastrously wrong due to a few major oversights.

1. We did not clearly define its mission.
2. We did not clearly define its user base.
3. We did not have the right people running the project from the product or the technical side.
4. We departed from our mission of keeping it simple.
5. Rather than putting out a lesser version sooner and receiving feedback sooner, we spent two years developing what we, myself included, thought would be a breakthrough new category of trading software. We were wrong.

Had the beta gone moderately well with its targeted users of program traders, we could have and would have continued investing in the platform. But our beta program discovered architectural and functionality problems, and during the time it took to develop the product, the overall size of the market for program trading declined. We would have had to invest a lot more money to complete our product so we could fight the embedded incumbents for some market share of a declining market. We had invested roughly $10 million into its development up to that point. We had to make a very tough call. We decided to pull the plug.

As our business continued to decline due to the ongoing recession and many self-inflicted wounds, the one bright spot—the example I held up as us taking control of our future, of turning around our fortunes—had blown up spectacularly. Roughly 10 percent of our staff had spent two years of their lives working on the project, and it was the hope for our future. When we made the decision to close it down, it severely and understandably affected morale and my credibility. Employees started losing faith in our future and in my leadership. There had already been disenchantment with the leadership of the company that started with the recession and continued through some poor hiring decisions and declining bonuses. Now that we pulled the plug on our most exciting endeavor, our people saw Liquidnet as a sinking ship.

I quickly questioned the decision to pull Liquidnet 4.0 because of the dramatic impact on morale and the excruciating pain it caused throughout the company. Liquidnet employees' resumes were now scattered all over the street. Some of our best people quit. The company no longer had the luxury of losing money across multiple fronts. We had to protect the franchise, protect our core, and make sure we could live to fight another day.

With the benefit of hindsight, I now understand what the decision to pull a potentially great project cost us in terms of morale, but like many other missteps, I see it as a learning exercise and part of our trajectory to create subsequent products that were better because of that failure.

THE MISTAKES THAT DON'T KILL YOU . . .

Every company has its misses, its mistakes, its failures it wished it avoided. Consider Apple's famous Lisa. While a huge achievement technically, it wasn't a hit in the market. It cost Apple $50 million in hardware and $100 million in development, and it sold only 10,000 computers. Later, the Apple III was so unstable that it was pulled from the market and re-released a year later.[2] Microsoft has had more failures than successes, such as the Zune and the Windows phone, just to name the more recent ones, but the Windows operating system and Office bundle helps it survive its missteps. Even the hottest ventures like Elon Musk's Tesla and Space X had to suffer failed launches before getting it right.

When Even the Silver Lining Is Lead

Another adjacent, new business we were investing in, which I felt was ripe for disruption and I was very excited about, was equity capital markets. Equity capital markets refers to the issuance of new shares of a company's stock either via an initial public offering (IPO) or, if the company is already public, when they issue additional shares through what is called a secondary offering. Liquidnet had established the first electronic global distribution platform by virtue of having desktop presence at all the world's largest investors. I thought this could be an unfair competitive advantage.

There hadn't been any innovation in the capital markets space since capital markets were invented. Everyone knew that IPOs were, if not rigged, highly inefficient, as was the whole way that companies issued securities after the IPO. We could do much better leveraging technology, our global customer base, and our liquidity pool. It would be great for the issuers, as they would tap into the world's largest investors and it would be great for our members, as it would be a whole new source of liquidity. I was very bullish on this idea.

We did a deal partnering with the New York Stock Exchange. Again, like so much of what Liquidnet was built on, we found a way to use technology to create value propositions. We created a product called InfraRed that aggregated all our members' buy and sell orders into what we called an "institutional sentiment index."

It was pretty cool. With this offering we could go into a public company and tell them on an almost real-time basis what our membership (which constituted around 70 percent of the institutionally managed equity assets in the United States) were really thinking about their stock.[3] In aggregate, are they buying it or are they selling it? We vetted the idea with our members first, as it was their data and the vast majority agreed to have their information included. With InfraRed, we were able to provide the New York Stock Exchange and public companies with information that no one else could give them, and it gave us entry into this new customer segment. We hired a team to market the product, and within two years we signed up more than 600 public companies.

We didn't charge for InfraRed, but it had the potential to be a huge revenue generator. There were 600 public companies that had never heard of Liquidnet that now knew who we were and what we did. Within a very short time frame, we had 600 prospects for our capital markets business and growing. The expectation we set for using our software was when these public companies did a stock buyback or secondary offering, we would be included in it. And it was starting to work. But just as we started to win a small amount of business for the capital markets business, we received a subpoena from the Securities and Exchange Commission (SEC).

We as a firm pride ourselves as being above reproach. We aspire to set the example for honesty and integrity on Wall Street. There were no gray areas for us; there was either right or wrong. Receiving a subpoena shook us to our core.

Liquidnet is both a broker-dealer and an alternative trading system (ATS). The rules that apply to an ATS are different from those of a broker-dealer, especially when it comes to sharing data. We were always careful about protecting our members' information as their trust in us was the core to our success, and loss of that trust would be the end of our business.

As the capital markets business got going, and we had more interaction with public companies, some of the folks in the capital markets group started taking more liberties with what data they shared with the companies. They came from traditional broker-dealers where that kind of information sharing was routine. For example, they would share descriptive characteristics, saying, "There was a large asset manager in the Midwest that bought your stock today or sold your stock today." They didn't think they were revealing too much—or doing anything wrong—because they weren't giving out the names. And the capital market's customers, the issuers, were appreciative of this information.

I found out about this in an alarming and unpleasant way—when the SEC came for a routine audit and uncovered it. The SEC also found that in the course of running and supporting the capital markets business, the capital markets salespeople had access to data that we had not properly disclosed to our members.

As an offense to be accused of, this came as a surprise to me. We had fully disclosed everything about InfraRed to our members. They had expressed that they were comfortable with it, and we had also given them the ability to opt out in case they were not. As we were building additional functionality for our capital markets team, we gave the team more and more access to information so that they could make better calls to our corporate prospects. We didn't see a problem with sharing this information with them; it was the information they needed to help them know which prospects to pursue in order to bring the liquidity into our system that the members wanted.

That presented an unusual problem. We shared aggregated member information with some of our capital markets prospects that was broader than we had disclosed to our members, which we never should have done. From a regulatory perspective, according to our lawyers, we had not violated any regulatory policies by sharing information internally, but we did violate our internal policy.

Tell the Truth

SEC investigations are not made public, and every company facing this type of examination does its best to keep it a secret for as long as possible and preferably until either a fine is assessed or no action is taken.

We had a very different relationship with our customers, so while we did not have much information to share, we decided that we should tell our members that we had received a subpoena. It was highly unusual and our lawyers advised us against it, but given our commitment to honesty and transparency, we decided to self-disclose even before we had done our own investigation to gauge the severity of the problem.

Being honest and transparent includes being open and honest even when things go wrong—and especially when things go wrong. At every orientation I tell new employees, "Look, you've got to tell the truth. You're not perfect. We're not perfect. Get the bad news out there quickly."

I had to follow my own advice and set the path forward for our company. This is when values really count, as making this disclosure at the very start of the investigation was a critical risk to the entire firm. There were no discoveries yet, there were no findings, and we could not tell our members how bad or benign we thought this would be.

We wrote a letter to our members alerting them to the investigation. Then I made a bunch of phone calls to members before the letter went out, to test their reaction to the letter. And then we shared it with the press—*Bloomberg*, the *Wall Street Journal*, the *Financial Times*, and others. We called a number of industry analysts to brief them on the situation, and made them aware that they were going to get calls. We invited members to come in for a visit. We said, "We welcome you to come to our office and see our operations and what we do." We hosted them for a full day or a half-day and let them see how we protect their data.

The biggest question that we had to answer was, "Is there anything more?"

Our answer to that was the difficult truth: "We don't know yet." That only made them more concerned.

That was all that we could say. And that was hard for our members as it created additional potential risks to the confidentiality of their information and it put us in a very difficult position with them. We shared what we knew in the moment, and we assured them that we would keep them informed. We believed that disclosing the investigation ourselves was the right thing to do; it was in line with our core values and our relationships with our members.

While it was the right thing to do, it wasn't the easy thing to do. We were embarrassed. We held ourselves up as the firm that is the ethical standard on Wall Street. This significantly damaged the trust our members had in us, which we had worked hard to build.

Our disclosure could have been the end of Liquidnet, and there was a period of time after the disclosure where we had to gauge whether Liquidnet would stay in business. The vast majority of our members understood and stuck by us, but there were about 30 firms—some small and some of the largest—that stopped doing business with us immediately. The disclosures and tough conversations took a toll on everyone in the firm, but especially those on the front lines, the salespeople and leadership. If our people thought the ship was sinking before this, this tore a huge gaping hole in our hull. We embarrassed our members who were loyal to us, we lost our status as squeaky clean, we lost business, and we opened the door for our competition. Those members who felt they didn't need more than one institutional crossing network now felt a responsibility to not be beholden and rely solely on us. This was truly our brush with death.

We knew the risk of self-disclosing, but we had no idea how long it would take the SEC to finish their investigation and issue their report, so we had no idea how much it would ultimately cost the firm. It cost us dearly from a reputational and revenue perspective. The investigation took two years to complete. In that two years we lost about $20 million in revenue and spent around $6 million in legal fees, not to mention the countless hours spent in discovery and depositions. We were fined $2 million, and in the end the SEC admitted that no harm was done to any of our members.

So was self-disclosing the right thing to do? One hundred percent it was. *Standing by your core values is not always easy, but I believe the tough times are when they are needed most.* I firmly believe that because of the way we handled this life-or-death situation, our members will trust us to be completely honest with them in the future for all things good and bad.

When Nothing Will Ever Be the Same

It was a brutal time, a dire time. It was a constant onslaught of self-inflicted and market-related disasters. There was no light at the end of the tunnel, and it seemed the tunnel had no end. We were a firm that went from transforming the industry and having the Midas touch to a firm that could not get anything right. Even our members lost faith in us.

It was during this dark period, on January 31, 2014, that I was in a board meeting when my assistant came in and handed me a note. My wife, Anne, who was in Florida for the weekend competing in a horse jumping competition had fallen off her horse. Anne was a very competitive rider and had broken just about every bone in her body at some point. This kind of news was unfortunate but not uncommon. I got in touch with Anne's parents, who were in Florida watching her compete, to see how bad it was. They were on their way to the hospital and said they would call when they got there.

About half an hour later, Anne's father called, crying. Anne's brain was swelling and the doctors had to remove part of her skull to relieve it. The doctor asked if Anne had a living will. It was only then that I left the board meeting to head to the airport. I told my father-in-law I would call before the plane took off. I called as I was boarding the plane, but it was neither my father-in-law nor mother-in-law who answered. An unfamiliar voice started talking, "Anne came in with severe head trauma; we did everything that we could . . ."

My beautiful wife, whom I met on the kibbutz the year after high school, my life partner, mother of my three kids, and my soul mate, had died on the operating table.

The Worst of Crises Can Fuel the Fight

At the time of the accident, Anne and I were talking about slowing down at work and spending more time together. Our kids were grown. She was going to transition the leadership of her philanthropic organization to someone else on the board, and I was going to delegate more to the other executives at Liquidnet. Together, we would follow the sun: to Florida, Israel, and Westchester.

That plan no longer made sense. Working hard no longer made any sense, either. Why do any of it if Anne wasn't going to be here to help me enjoy the results of it? I had no anchor.

Everyone I knew called to take me to dinner. I dreaded every encounter and the kind of conversations we would have, but I dreaded being by myself even more. The one thing I didn't want to be was alone.

I needed to go back to work in order to keep myself busy and keep my sanity. And I needed to turn the company around or I would be letting Anne down. Anne had been intimately involved at Liquidnet. A superstar lawyer by training and off-the-charts smart, we talked about every problem I faced or major decision I made. She created the philanthropic arm of Liquidnet, Liquidnet for Good, and ran our signature program, the Agahozo Shalom Youth Village (ASYV), a village in Rwanda for orphans, where many of our employees volunteered. She knew everyone at the company and everyone knew her. She played such a key role that we had talked about how if anything happened to me, she would step in as chairperson.

But now it was I who had to step up. This is the moment where I learned that you have no idea what is inside you, what you are capable of, how much you can bear until you actually have to do it. I threw myself into fixing the company with everything I had. I had to succeed for Anne and for my kids.

I dove in completely at work. For the next two years, I was on a plane just about every other day. I worked nonstop. I soon learned that all the clichés and platitudes about "what doesn't kill you makes you stronger" or "it's not how hard you fall, but how fast you get up" are incredibly *un*helpful when the company is down for the count, but are incredibly true if you can pick yourself up and find the will and the energy to do what is necessary to turn the company around.

One of the toughest days immediately after the accident was when Liquidnet held a memorial service for Anne. It was the first time I had seen my coworkers since the accident, and I felt the profound shift from being "Seth the CEO" to "Seth who just lost his wife." Many people got up and shared stories about Anne and they cried. I was crying in front of the company, even though I tried not to. But seeing how much everyone cared, and understanding how much I cared about them, made me grateful for the kind of company we had built. We were more than cogs in a wheel; we were a group of people who mattered to one another.

There were too many awesome people who devoted a good part of their waking lives to Liquidnet to stay down. In addition to a tremendous amount of skill and talent, we had strengths and advantages that we could build upon. We could have sold out, we could have taken on a strategic investor, both of which were discussed in board meetings, but both would have been admitting defeat. It was unbelievably tough to deal with everything that hit the company and me personally, but giving up felt like everything that had happened would have been for nothing. There would have been no meaning to any of it.

We got to work. We built an entirely new global technology framework that could harness our data, keep track of it, manage it, and provide safeguards of member information to prevent another SEC situation from occurring again. We reduced the number of priorities in the company to three: expand the core, grow our algorithmic business, and diversify our revenue base by expanding into fixed-income trading. We had specific tactics for each of the priorities, and we talked about these three priorities until everyone in the company could recite them. Everyone knew if they were not working on one of these priorities, they were working on the wrong things.

In order to grow our algorithmic business, we fired many of the people who ran the business and hired a whole new team of experienced quants and electronic trading executives to redo our entire algorithmic suite. We rebuilt our global trading technology, and to focus on our core, we promoted a young but brilliant person from the product team to run the product group to finish and deliver our new Liquidnet 5 platform. Then we acquired an electronic fixed-income brokerage firm to launch our fixed-income business. We had to get everything perfect from here. We simply could not afford any more mistakes. The only way we had a shot at coming back was to do just a few things and do them flawlessly.

Notes

1. Fred Yager, "The Cost of Bad Hiring Decisions Runs High." *Dice.* insights.dice.com/report/the-cost-of-bad-hiring-decisions/
2. Chandra Steele, "7 Steve Jobs Products that Failed." *PC* magazine, August 26, 2011; www.pcmag.com/slideshow/story/286886/7-steve-jobs-products-that-failed
3. This was an opt-in feature where members had to agree to include their information in the product. The information was provided on a nonidentifiable, aggregated basis so our members' trading intentions and information were kept confidential.

11

Culture by Design or Culture by Default

Another lesson I learned the hard way: Don't wait to decide what kind of culture you wish to have in your company. Determine it at the beginning and then design it, implement it, teach it, and lead by example. If you don't, your company will have a culture, but it will be a culture by default. That might be good or it might be bad, but it will not be of your making. A strong culture is critical to long-term success, but only in a crisis will you find out how important culture is in the short term.

The financial crisis, while brutal for our business, didn't kill us. My family crisis, while personally devastating, didn't destroy us. But something else almost did—a culture crisis that sharply divided the firm in two.

As we were entering the economic downturn, we hired a group of incredibly smart and hard-working people who had previously been at a large bulge bracket bank. They brought a lot of experience that we were lacking in many areas of our business—especially the algorithmic business—and we believed their skills would bring great value to our firm. As they got to work, it was clear they truly did possess talent and experience where we were lacking and they brought a new sense of urgency and work ethic to the firm.

However, about a year into the group's tenure, I started hearing about some worrisome issues. As opposed to working as one Liquidnet team, this new unit was choosing to fiercely compete against other departments and other teams. Instead of helping other areas and groups succeed, they made sure resources were not available to them in an effort to ensure that any other projects would fail. It became clear this wasn't just something coming from a few paranoid employees; the new team actually told people they would make sure other departments would fail. I assume they believed they were so smart and productive that they would become indispensable and they could take over more of the firm. I assume they also thought that in order for them to succeed others had to fail.

This, of course, was counter to everything we believed in and the culture we had built. It seemed incredible to me that people could be so bold and ruthless about their personal goals at the expense of others in the firm.

This team was very loyal to those people who reported to them, and as a result, they had very ardent supporters. At the same time, the team tried to crush anyone not on its team. They viewed everyone else at Liquidnet as the opposition. Those not on their team grew to resent the newcomers and the dangerous power they wielded. Needless to say, this resulted in a very toxic environment. We were reeling from disappointments and disasters, so the firm was divided into those who thought they were exactly what Liquidnet needed and those who believed they were further destroying Liquidnet.

The firm was becoming polarized around this group, with many people saying, "If they go, we go," and just as many saying, "If they don't go, we will." Everyone knew that the situation had to be resolved and was looking to see which way I would go. Would I let this star team go? Or would I keep them and promote them to run all of development as they wished. In either case, we knew we would lose people—up to half of our developers who were loyal to one faction or the other.

If You Don't Fully Trust Employees, Let Them Go

I asked our human resources team to dig in and do a more in-depth investigation and come back to me with a recommendation. Their findings were that the concern was overblown, that they were not as bad as people were saying, and that they were incredibly productive. Their recommendation was to bite the bullet and put the new team in charge of all of development.

As I was considering the recommendation, I had to admit that while they were smart and savvy, they didn't reflect the values of the firm or the culture we had built. This presented the classic dilemma of do you keep the really talented people at the expense of your culture, or do you stay true to your culture and in our case, the "no asshole" rule? Furthermore, I had a moment where I feared that if we parted ways, they could possibly do something terrible, like plant something malicious into our code base. I knew that if I had even an inkling of that concern, I clearly did not trust them. That cemented the decision for me: they had to go.

There was so much anxiety within the company leading up to the decision and worry over the two dramatically different possible outcomes—whether we would part ways or whether they would be put in charge of all of technology. I asked the team to come to a meeting the morning of my decision, and no one in the firm knew which way it would go except for HR and me. The team was shown the door and left Liquidnet that day.

Almost immediately after the decision was made, there was a collective sigh of relief throughout the organization. Within a couple of weeks of their departure, the mood around the company went from dark to almost exuberant. It was as if a black cloud that was the source of all the tension had parted and given way to light. That was a huge confirmation that I made the right decision.

People no longer felt they had to look over shoulders or be so protective of their work. They began to enjoy their jobs again and flourished. I realized that for too long we had been working against each other—fighting against ourselves instead of the enemy. When we demonstrated—through action—that we were serious about our core values and our culture, we became a newly united organization. People worked collaboratively again, and many stepped up and took on more responsibility, and productivity soared. In the end, only a few people left, and those who stayed proved to be pure Liquidnet people who exhibited our values and were in pursuit of the same collective corporate goals.

Determining the kind of company you want to build and the culture you want to create is one of the most important decisions you can make. A culture has to be envisioned, crafted, and created. It has to be taught, lived, demonstrated, and upheld. Any deviation from the top will invalidate the values. Any act that is counter to the culture has to be noted and dealt with immediately. It is very easy to overlook or forgive certain lapses in your culture, but while culture can be taught, it is implemented only through action and living it every day. Each lapse diminishes the culture a bit. Many lapses or prolonged failure to fix a lapse in culture can destroy it.

During our culture crisis, I saw the value of our strong culture, and out of that strength grew what I call our efficient organ-rejection mechanism. If we hire someone that does not fit our culture, it becomes obvious to people around that person way faster than it does to those of us in leadership. People who work with that person form the antibodies identifying the foreign object, and that filters up to leadership fairly quickly and we take steps to fix it. If we can't fix it, we reject it. That mechanism protects the whole system. Only in a strong, well-understood culture will everyone be able to identify people that fit and people that don't. Too many times a bad hire can stay around for way too long, causing morale issues or poor work habits that affect all those around them, but an efficient organ-rejection mechanism helps protect against that.

FIRING IS JUST AS IMPORTANT AS HIRING

Running a company successfully is a lot like being a coach of a sports team. Like any great coach, your goal is to win the championship or be the best in your field. To do so, like a coach, you have to have rigorous standards for who's on the team and who's not. There might be some folks that just don't show up for practice or show up for practice and put in the minimal amount of effort. You want to win the championship? Those people have to go. There might be some folks who show up to all the practices but they just don't have the skills. You want to win the championship? Those people have to go, too.

If you really want to be the best in the world, you have to have not only the best players in the world but those who can work together as a team. They must have the aptitude, the willingness to put the time in to train, prepare, and execute, and the desire and passion to win. Be strict with your standards, be diligent and constant about weeding out those that are not or cannot be the best in the world.

Admit the Brutal Facts

Pulling ourselves out of the many crises that hit us meant that we had to admit that we had serious problems—face them and fix them. We focused on our biggest problems first, declining revenue in the U.S. and European regions.

We had to significantly upgrade our hiring process to ensure that every new hire was a great hire, which is detailed later in this chapter. We used the new hiring process to hire Brennan Warble as the new head of U.S. sales. Within two years, the U.S. sales staff had changed by almost 60 percent. Boston, our biggest region in the United States, was a big problem. It had the highest potential, but we were doing terribly. We needed a new leader there. We used our interviewing and hiring process—benchmarking the characteristics of the best salespeople, looking for those traits through personality tests and an intensive interview process. It worked and we found Tracy Windham, the perfect internal candidate. Tracy had moved from Liquidnet U.S. to Liquidnet Asia-Pac eight years before as a relationship manager and grew to run all of sales in the region—which she did very effectively. We brought her back to run Boston. We folded Canada, which was its own region, and underperforming, into a new "Americas region," with everyone reporting to Brennan. The Canada business is up significantly year over year since we made the change.

We hired a new head of Europe, Mark Pumfrey, a leader who didn't come with an electronic trading background, but who met the criteria of what we benchmarked for a successful managing director. We put a lot of effort into the search. He interviewed with more than 20 people and received unanimous support. He was the right fit and has grown the European business materially in three years.

Hiring more effectively and accurately was crucially important, and the successful hires helped to turn the company around. But there was so much more to do. We used to joke at the conclusion of leadership off-sites that we were focused on 12 of our top 10 priorities. The problem was that it was true. There is no way you can focus on so many priorities at once and do them all flawlessly. We had to stop that ridiculousness. Coming out of the crisis, we altered our strategy to focus on three things, as mentioned in the previous chapter.

First, we would focus on our core business, global block trading. That's still the bulk of our business. We needed to focus on growing this foundation, and did so by expanding into new markets such as Taiwan and India. We also grew it by enhancing the amount of liquidity with new products and adding new members and new sources of liquidity, such as venture capitalists and private equity firms, to expand on our lead as the largest, most diversified pool of block liquidity.

Second, we focused on new business areas, such as the execution and quantitative strategies (EQS) business—the algorithmic business—which leverages our global platform and offers a much larger opportunity than our core business. We want to win at what-ever we do, and we want to be the best in the world at it. We were not the best in the world at the algorithmic business and we knew that. Facing the brutal facts gave us the urgency to change our strat-egy there. We brought in a new person to head that business, Rob Laible, who spent his whole career in electronic trading. Rob quickly built a new team. We re-architected the entire global trading tech-nology infrastructure and built a new algorithmic suite. It's resulted in record growth. We launched in Asia-Pac in the first half of 2016 and expect similar success.

Third, we focused on diversifying our revenue. We acquired a small fixed-income company called Vega-Chi. We already had all the largest asset managers globally as members. The most profitable business strategy is to sell more products to existing customers, so we made some enhancements to the platform, plugged the new com-pany into our distribution system, and about a year and a half later flipped the switch and should break even within a year. It's been a fast-growing, high-potential diversification of revenue strategy. Entering the fixed-income business has begun our transition to a broad, global, diversified financial services firm.

In each of these turnarounds we stuck to strategies we'd seen work before. We established a client base and expanded it by sell-ing more products into that base, and we made sure that we had an unfair competitive advantage in each new business we entered. Our EQS business had to be better than the existing offerings, and we made it so by leveraging our strength of having desktop space on every trader's desk and access to the largest, most diverse pool of liquidity. In fixed income, we created an unfair competitive advan-tage by leveraging our customer base and technology to do some-thing that was never done before—centralizing all fixed-income liquidity in one institutional pool: ours.

Hire Partners, Not Employees

In surviving crises and executing a comeback, I learned that hiring is the most important thing to get right. After many, *many* mistakes, we have honed a hiring process that we feel really good about and has resulted in many more fits than not.

As we learned with the team hire from the large bulge bracket firm, not everyone is a fit for Liquidnet, and Liquidnet is not a fit for everyone. So how did we figure out who will succeed here? We look to hire people who have four passions: a passion for their work, a passion for Liquidnet, a passion to continue to learn and improve, and a passion to win. Employees must have the ability, the determination, and the work ethic to be the best in the world at what they do. If they're most interested in the amount of money they'll earn, the amount of vacation time they'll get, or the title they'll receive, those are red flags that this candidate may not be the right cultural fit. We benchmark the character and personality traits of the best people we have in the roles that we need to fill and ask that every candidate take two personality tests to see how close they are to our benchmark employee's traits.

We are very clear that we're not looking for employees—we're looking for partners. That means that we expect everyone to share and live our core values, to always do what's in the best interest of the company, and we hold everyone accountable to be awesome at what they do. There's a lot of reinforcement of that. We give everyone at Liquidnet stock or options so that they feel invested in this company. It works. Partners take more responsibility for the whole enterprise as opposed to only their role within it. The benefits range from a constant flow of suggestions for how we can improve the company and our products to people looking more critically at their own expenses as well as what's spent in the company because they see it as their money. We want partners who feel responsible for the good of the whole organization.

HOW TO HIRE THE RIGHT PARTNERS

We tell people we're not looking for employees, mercenaries, or people who want a "job." We're looking for people who are really smart and really want to make a difference in the world and who see that as their mission.

To that end, we've honed and greatly refined our interview process:

- **Step 1: Create the interview team.** The number of people on the team depends on the position. A senior management position might include everyone on leadership, as many as 16 to 20 people. A position for a developer may have 5 or 6 people on the team.

- **Step 2: Team huddle.** Everyone must understand the requirements of the position, what they are looking for in the candidate, and be in alignment. The team goes over the formal job spec and discusses characteristics, traits, and experience required. This coordination is essential. Frequently in job searches, various people interview a candidate, each looking for different things. That means some people will reject candidates for the same reasons someone else wants to hire them. In our process, the team divides up the characteristics, traits, and experience they will probe for during the interview.

- **Step 3: Ask the right questions.** Every manager at Liquidnet has been trained on behavioral interviewing skills. You don't really learn much by asking the same interview questions that the candidate has been prepped for: "If there's one thing to improve upon, what would that be?" . . . "Tell me something you're very proud of." Everyone is prepared to answer the conventional interview questions. (The one thing they'd improve is changing the way they "take on too much" or are "too much of a perfectionist".) Instead, behavioral interviewing skills rely on a series of questions that help to understand how the candidate thinks and reacts to situations. This process, and the way they answer the series of questions, is analyzed to provide better insight into the fit of that candidate for a specific role.

- **Step 4: Determine if there is a cultural fit.** You have to know whether and how someone will fit into the company. We have a three-page list of interview questions designed to determine how they think about accountability, honesty, problem solving, listening, and more. I have included sample questions in the Appendix on page 193 but some examples include:

  - What would you do if you saw another employee acting out at a networking event and it clearly was not in the best interest of the company?

  - It is goal-setting time. You and your boss have set some exciting goals for you and your team. You then realize, given the existing workload and bandwidth, that these are more "nice to have" than must-haves. How do you handle this?

  - Describe the corporate culture of your last two to three employers. What worked? What didn't?

  - Tell me about a time when you made a mistake and someone was blamed for your error. How did you handle it?

- **Step 5: Make sure they have the right personality traits for the job.** We give every candidate two personality exams, one that tests their emotional quotient (EQ), such as their passion and softer side, and another that looks to understand their character traits to see what strengths and weaknesses they bring to the table. Not everyone on the team has to have certain traits—and having a mix is vital—but there are certain characteristics that we have benchmarked that determine success in different roles, and knowing whether the candidate is strong or weak in those characteristics offers another helpful data point. For example, if someone is seeking a role in data analytics and doesn't possess the analytics gene, then it's a

problem; or if someone is pursuing sales and is not amiable, they might
not be cut out for the role.

- **Step 6: Make a unanimous decision.** At the end of the interviewing process, the team huddles together again to discuss the candidate. Only if
  everyone is in agreement do we offer the candidate a job.

No Titles . . .

Getting the right people in the door is one thing, but keeping them
is another. What do great people want? Figuring that out is the
secret to attracting and retaining the right people and providing
them long-term opportunities.

We were never really that into titles at Liquidnet, but within the
development organization, the largest department, titles started to
become a big deal. There were many different levels and a clear
hierarchy to the roles. While it wasn't quite as bad as a bank where
there's an associate vice president, vice president, executive vice
president, super executive vice president, and so on, we started seeing our own "title creep" come in. People we were recruiting were
fixated on what title they would be given and our existing people
were hyper-focused on being promoted to the next title.

We found that having titles and people aspiring to get to the
next title wasn't really helping the company. It was helping individuals build their resumes, but it wasn't helping them build Liquidnet.
That was a problem because our allegiance is to the company, not
the individual.

By investigating it further, we discovered that titles themselves
inherently carry a lot of problems. For starters, titles are a class system of tenure and seniority. That means that titles create divides.
We felt that titles prevented or inhibited people from offering their
opinions in a meeting. We didn't want to have a situation where an
associate sitting at a table with an executive VP was scared to speak
their mind because there was an executive VP in the room.

We decided we would eliminate all titles. Rather than people
aspiring to attain a higher title, I wanted people to aspire to take on
more responsibility. More responsibility is better for the company
and therefore should get them more recognition and be better for
their careers at Liquidnet.

It's complete common sense, but it was very controversial when I announced we would eliminate all titles. To most of the people at the company it was received well because it was "very Liquidnet." (Translation: very different from Wall Street.) But to a few people it was of great concern. *How will we be able to attract people if we don't offer them a good title? If we change jobs, how do we know whether it's a lateral move or a step up? If everybody in the department has the same business card, how will vendors know to whom they should be talking?*

Abandoning titles served as a self-selection mechanism. It actually helped us attract the right people. If title is what's really important to someone, then this was not the right place for him or her. It also helped speed up the onboarding process since title was no longer an issue to be negotiated. As far as vendors being confused, that didn't manifest at all. We explained the reasons we were eliminating titles and our people understood that we wanted everyone's viewpoint no matter how senior or junior they were, and if they really wanted to get ahead at the company, they should look to take on more responsibility over time.

Having no titles is more than symbolic. Leveling the playing field in this way *has* elevated everyone's involvement. Everyone understands they have a voice and they are not afraid to speak up in any situation. The power of tapping everyone's brains in the company has been tremendous.

Just to give you one example: One time I was in a meeting proposing an idea I was very excited about. The room was filled. There was one person, an intern, who was still in college and just with us for the summer. He disagreed with me and spoke up against my idea. He very clearly articulated why it didn't make sense and he made such a good case that I agreed with him right there in the meeting. He was right and his speaking up ultimately saved the company a lot of time. Great ideas come from everywhere, people just have to be empowered to share them and everyone has to be open to listening.

HOW TO IMPLEMENT A NO TITLE POLICY

The elimination of titles is meant to ensure that everyone feels comfortable stating their opinion in any meeting. Remove titles and tell your people that instead of aspiring to a title, they will advance their careers by aspiring to take on more responsibility. People will still have managers. We organize roles internally by the level of responsibility you have in the company:

- **Shapes**. Most of the folks on the leadership team are shapes. We help shape the direction of the company. This person is a highly visible leader:
  - Considered an expert within the industry/discipline.
  - Provides broad external perspective and brings innovative ideas and thought leadership to effect change across the organization.
  - Makes decisions that have significant impact on the company's revenue, cost, and profitability.
  - Sets strategic objectives for the entire company.
  - Significantly influences the company's strategy, vision, and core values.
  - Has autonomy to determine resources, organizational structure.
  - Accountable for setting, managing, and achieving budget.
  - Influences resource allocation decisions across the company.
  - Develops and mentors future leaders of the company.
  - Proactively identifies and solves unique and complex problems that have a broad impact on the management and the direction of the business.
  - Works with multiple disciplines and resources to drive solutions to complex business issues.
- **Guides.** Manage significant external business relationships and partnerships or are considered a thought leader in a discipline. This leader:
  - Works independently, with guidance in only the most complex situations.
  - Solves unique and complex problems and makes decisions with impact on multiple areas/departments.
  - Takes a broad perspective to identify innovative solutions.
  - Understands the industry and implications of changes on the company's business.
  - Influences others (including senior leaders) to adopt different or new concepts.
  - Drives multidisciplinary projects with significant complexity to achieve strategic objectives.
- **Drives.** Work independently with broad oversight. This person manages external business relationships/partnerships or is considered a subject-matter expert and acts as a resource for colleagues. He or she:
  - Understands the department's impact on the company and its role in the industry.

- Creates and validates solutions for complex problems within a delegated set of objectives.

- Makes complex decisions independently that make an impact at the department level.

- Takes ownership for resolving issues across departments.

- Effectively communicates with and can raise issues throughout the company as necessary.

- Explains complex issues and works to build understanding within the department.

- Manages specific project deliverables at the department level.

- Requires technical expertise in the area managed or has a strong knowledge of a related discipline that is sufficient to accomplish tasks, specific initiatives, and decisions for the team.

- **Solves.** Require minimal supervision and direction to accomplish core job objectives. This person:

  - Is fully proficient in company-specific knowledge, interdependencies of departments, and impact of own role in company.

  - Has expanded knowledge, experience, and skills within own discipline.

  - Identifies and solves a range of problems with limited direction within own discipline using functional expertise and industry knowledge; escalates more complex issues if necessary.

  - Makes decisions within guidelines and policies that impact own group.

  - Serves as an information resource outside of team; influences fellow team members.

  - Validates individual schedule to achieve objectives and meet deadlines with team.

  - Is accountable for contribution to project team or subteam.

- **Creates.** Receive instruction, guidance, and direction from others. This team member:

  - Has strong foundational knowledge/experience within own discipline.

  - Provides solutions to moderately complex issues with limited direction; may gather information to help arrive at an appropriate solution.

  - Makes decisions that impact own priorities and allocation of time to meet deadlines.

  - Effective communicator within department; asks questions and checks for understanding.

  - Participates actively in achieving project-specific tasks.

GIVE FEEDBACK OFTEN

Not having titles does not mean we don't have big expectations of our people . . . we do. Everyone is accountable. We have a semiannual performance management review process and categorize people's performance in three levels. These levels are easy to understand and tend to encourage more honest feedback. These levels map to bonuses and future opportunities within the company. They enable us to constantly identify future leaders to cultivate, and low performers to remove, all of which is necessary to create a winning organization.

- **Awesome.** You have to go above and beyond what your daily responsibilities are. For example, someone would be "awesome" if a coworker had left or been let go and they proactively took on those additional responsibilities. Or if something came up that created unexpected additional work, perhaps around a regulatory issue and that person managed to execute their work and the additional unexpected work within their deadline. Or if a programmer who, in addition to their work, discovered a way to enhance the speed or functionality of the product and took on the responsibility to implement it. There are three categories we look for—"Results," "Engagement," "Fit & Skills"—and you need to get an awesome in all three categories to be an awesome overall. Ten percent of the organization on average reaches this status and everyone in leadership around the world knows who's been rated an "awesome." We want leadership to know the high-potential people and we want to train them and provide them with opportunities to grow.

- **Successful.** About 80 to 85 percent of the organization falls into this category. This does not mean that most of the company does an average job. A successful employee consistently delivers high-quality results on time and on plan and meets the expected standards for the position and role. He or she is viewed as responsible, reliable, and one who goes above and beyond to meet objectives. Being successful means they are doing a great job. This employee is a true asset to the company.

- **Improvement required.** If you get "improvement required" in two out of three categories, you receive an overall improvement required. No one should ever be surprised at review time because managers should not wait for reviews to provide feedback. Feedback should be constant. Your manager has to be able to tell you what it is that needs improvement as well as what you need to do to meet expectations. Up to 10 percent get this. If it happens twice, there's a serious discussion about whether you stay at the firm. But if we are doing our job well, the person and the company will part ways long before we have to give them an improvement required for a second time. The manager should have seen that they are not improving and started the process to move them out of the firm.

No Ties . . .

Unlike the rest of the financial world, Liquidnet has a no-suits-and-no-ties mandate. Like not having titles in a world where titles are status symbols, mandating no ties or suits around the office or at client meetings is an important visual and social statement of informality we feel benefits the workplace, interpersonal relationships within the company, and, even more importantly, with our customers. I want to encourage casual and friendly interaction between people, which is just too hard when people are dressed formally. When we're sitting around in jeans, or whatever people want to wear, that's the kind of interaction I want.

We have much closer relationships with our members than do people at other firms I believe in part due to our dress code. There are many things within our firm's culture that enables us to have closer relationships with our members but we relate to our members much more casually and more as friends than people at other firms in part due to our casual dress code.

. . . and No Assholes

At every new employee orientation we explain that we have a clear "No Asshole Policy" here. We all work together. There's no backstabbing, no territoriality, no hoarding of information. If we see bureaucracy creep in, we try our best to stamp it out. Everybody should be invested and working in the same direction and pulling as one team.

It's very important that people understand we have a zero tolerance policy. It doesn't matter how good you are, if you're an asshole, you're going to get fired. This is much harder to adhere to than one might think. You have to be extremely disciplined in upholding this policy, especially when you have a super-smart and productive employee who just can't get along with other people or has a different set of values or priorities than the company. But disciplined you must be: even if it hurts in the short run, it is critical in the long run.

Having this unusually stated policy in place has provided clear direction for everybody in all of our offices, all around the world. Managers have permission—and a blessing—to get rid of folks who cause problems with their teams. The people who work here now are talented and good-hearted. When people like what they do, like who they work with, and share the same values, you don't spend time on the negatives and your productivity soars and your opportunities are only limited by your imagination.

Invest in People

People remain excited about their jobs when they are continually learning and growing in their roles. Investing in your employees, providing training programs, funds for coursework, and mentors who can help them develop their skills is good for business. I don't understand how some companies that don't train their employees think that everyone they hire is the best possible version they can be. How can you be the best team if you're not constantly training, practicing, and improving?

Investing in training our employees is investing in our company for the long term. Our people love that we invest in their education and we love that having better-trained people raises the game throughout the company. It also says that our people are not simply cogs in a wheel. They are very important to us and we want to train them to continue to be the best that they can possibly be.

To this end, we created a budget per employee for external education and conferences and started Liquidnet University to develop very tailored training courses. The type of courses we handle internally are more soft skills, including courses on presentation training, management skills, sales skills, negotiation, and leadership skills. Liquidnet University also develops the intensive training programs we put new senior-level employees through. If we do not have the in-house expertise, then we supplement with the external resources and encourage our people to sign up for external courses that will help them do their jobs or grow into new responsibilities. Recently, we've gone another step above that and partnered with New York University to create a mini-master's degree for our high-potential talent. We've identified talent at all levels, all over the world, and we fly them in for three intense one-week programs, over the course of a year and a half at NYU, where they get an advanced crash course in the financial industry, business management, financial management, marketing, and strategy, among other subjects. All classes are selected in partnership with NYU and tailored specifically to our company.

But being happy at work is also about allowing people to have fun. I love that you can be in or walk past any meeting and there will always be some laughter. We want to ensure that people like who they work with and enjoy their time here. To that end, we create opportunities for them to build camaraderie. It starts with our office space. Every office around the world has the same design (and looks very different from a typical Wall Street firm's offices). We designed the offices to be open and bright with many communal spaces where people can congregate. We have large cafes in the center of the offices, and the fridges are always stocked with soft drinks and beer and the café is always filled with snacks, so much so that it looks like a small grocery store. But we don't charge anyone—it's all theirs. We want them to feel a sense of ownership. Every Friday we cater lunch. Several times a month we host different activities, like cake day to celebrate the birthdays that month; "Cheer," which is a contraction of cheese and beer night; and Quiz Night, where people socialize and have fun together.

Sometimes, when times are hard, as they were during the financial crisis, you have to measure the cost of providing these services relative to another hire. You have to make tough choices about what to cut. But I believe the decision rests on treating the people who continue to come to work every day in the best manner possible. Ultimately, it's not at all about snacks; it's about the whole package you present: it's your culture, it's your mission, it's how you lead. It is a competitive world out there, and you want the best people in the world, so you have to give them reasons to want to work at your company rather than somewhere else.

Your company is only as good as the people who work for it. Your value as a manager is based on the quality of the people on your team. I believe that every person makes a difference, and I want everyone to know that. That is why I personally meet every employee around the world—and I know their names and try to get to know them as people. It's why every Friday I invite a group of five or six employees to have lunch with me. It's why I write handwritten cards to everyone who's celebrating a three-year, five-year, or ten-year anniversary with the company. Every single person who works at Liquidnet is important and makes a difference. Everything that we do as a company and that I do as the CEO has to reflect that in actions, or else it is just words on paper somewhere.

Constant Improvement Must Be Part of the Culture

The reason I tell everyone during orientation that I'd much rather they assume that everything that we do here is wrong and part of their responsibility is to help us fix it is that I want everyone to know that we are on a constant drive to improve and everyone in the company has the responsibility to drive it. If it doesn't make sense to someone why we do something a certain way, question it. Maybe it's wrong. If you're growing quickly, what you did six months ago might have made complete sense, but today it doesn't.

One of the benefits of hiring new people is that if they have worked at other places, there has to be something that another firm does better than you and you should want to take advantage of those ideas. If everyone in the company knows they are responsible for constant improvement, there should be less ego and more willingness to try new ideas and acknowledge that there are things that you can do better.

I have always been afraid that being in the day-to-day will inhibit our ability to improve, innovate, and deliver new disruptive solutions to the market. This concern was immortalized in Clayton Christensen's book *The Innovator's Dilemma* (Harvard Business Review Press, 1997), which describes how successful companies all too often are completely focused on growing their business and solving their customers' current needs that they lose sight of the next disruption that might solve their customer's future problems. I never want my company to suffer the innovator's dilemma. We do have to continue to solve our customers' current needs, but there have to be some people who focus time and energy thinking about solutions beyond today's needs.

At Liquidnet, thinking about the future is primarily my responsibility. It is also my responsibility to withstand the pushback from the leadership team, who are accountable for the day-to-day and shorter-term goals. I have to push the company to allocate time and resources to deliver the next big thing that, if successful, might deliver revenue a few years down the road. I am religious about taking time to brainstorm new ideas, new processes, and new solutions to problems whether they are new product ideas, new marketing ideas, new ways to approach clients—anything and everything.

And since you can't brainstorm alone, I bring together people who are best able to brainstorm these ideas. Not everyone is good at brainstorming, and having those people in a brainstorming session is more disruptive than helpful. It's important to have creative people in the brainstorming group, and not all should be domain experts; involving people from different parts of the company gains different perspectives.

We have adopted a couple of brainstorming techniques at Liquidnet on which we provide training and for which we can provide facilitators. One simple methodology that we use often is called "divergent-convergent brainstorming." You pick a topic to brainstorm, and you go around the room writing down every idea that comes up without any critique or bias. That is the divergent part. Once all ideas have been delivered, you can give stickers or votes to each person to converge and pick the top three to five ideas. The ones with the most stickers or votes are the ideas that you drill into.

Our culture is to encourage new ideas and to cross-pollinate ideas. We try to eliminate all of our egos and listen to all suggestions and should be grateful when someone provides an idea that allows us to improve because everyone knows we'll succeed if we're on a continuing improvement cycle. By being self-critical and sharing ideas where we can improve, people are actually helping us.

This has enabled us to build a worldwide idea meritocracy. We have ideas coming from all over the world at an increasing pace. Most of our current new initiatives and products are now based on ideas that have come from people outside the leadership team. I view that statistic as an incredibly successful metric. Because of our focus on hiring great people, on continuous improvement and commitment to idea meritocracy, we have a very healthy pipeline of great ideas and we are able to implement and deliver those ideas faster and more consistently than our competition. This enables us to put greater distance between us and our competition around the world and since those ideas are being generated by lots of people involved in the business and not just me, I get to focus more of my time on the next big thing.

Repair the World

We say we want people who are passionate about their jobs, our company, and mission to make markets more efficient and a passion to continually improve. Our business has never just been about making money. If we can't make a market more efficient or apply technology to significantly improve some part of the market, we won't do it.

There was something else that was extremely important to me that I implemented as soon as we started to make some money. I believe every person and company has a higher purpose and that is to make the world a better place. The first responsibility I had was to make the company successful and profitable. Once I accomplished that I wanted Liquidnet to be *the* example of what corporate social responsibility could be. Not simply checkbook philanthropy, I wanted to make sure that we took on challenges that could change the world and make it a better place.

I believe that most people would like to give back in some way, but they either don't know how or are not given the opportunity to do so. I wanted Liquidnet to provide our employees with ways they can make the world a better place. We created Liquidnet for Good and hired a brilliant young person named Brian Walsh to run it full time. We followed the philosophy of *Tikkun olam*—the idea found in the Mishnah, a compilation of rabbinic teachings that we all have a responsibility to repair the world—and we embrace it.

When Anne and I first married, we used to talk about what we would do when we had money. We dreamed big. I wanted to be rich and she wanted to have enough money to buy horses and ride and then give the rest away. It was always a division of labor: I would make the money; she would give it away. And the more I made, the more she gave away.

But giving away money was never enough. We wanted to go way beyond just writing checks and using all of our resources for good. Anne was a former prosecutor in the Manhattan District Attorney's Office and brilliant in just about everything she did. She was the inspiration behind Liquidnet's philanthropic vision and programs. The person who we both thought was the most intelligent CEO of a large family foundation and to whom we both went for advice on our philanthropic goals later told me that Anne was the best philanthropist he had ever met. I wish he had told her that.

Anne developed and drove our biggest personal project and the signature project for Liquidnet, a youth village in the middle of Rwanda for orphans of the 1994 genocide. The Youth Village is named the Agahozo Shalom Youth Village (ASYV). Agahozo means a place where tears are dried in Kinyarwanda, and Shalom means peace in Hebrew. The village was inspired by the Israeli youth villages that provided homes for orphans from the Holocaust. The ASYV is a 144-acre campus that includes 32 homes, each housing 16 high school–age kids and a house mother, a high school, science and computer laboratories, sports fields, an organic farm, an 800-person cafeteria serving three meals a day, a reforestation program, and medical facilities.

This was initially a family endeavor, conceived of and executed by Anne, but the effort grew up with our company. Hundreds of Liquidnet employees from around the world, family members, and friends, through volunteer work, have contributed their time, resources, and passion; another 100 employees have visited the village to use their skills to turn this idea into a sustainable reality. Liquidnet employees have helped to set up human resource systems and procedures and an information technology infrastructure, implement accounting systems, install a wireless network throughout the village, create computer labs, and provide leadership training and staff development. Our employees have seen the village transform from a concept to blueprints to buildings to a village of 500 that the most vulnerable kids in the country call home.

The village has profoundly changed these kids' lives. In fact, it gave them lives. Kids who went from having absolutely nothing, from living on the streets, from having no home, no hope, and no future, to having brothers and sisters, access to the most modern facilities and teaching methods, sports teams, music and art teachers, and the highest scores in the country on their matriculation exams. Some 98.3 percent of them passed the National Secondary Exam; some 80 percent go to university on scholarships.

Doing this work changed our lives as well. It made us better people. It helped us attract the right people to the company and made our company better. Because of the programs, we truly have a higher purpose than simply making money and a higher purpose for the money we make.

I find that when we find the right people—people with this giving spirit—we can spark much more significant transformations and enjoy much more meaningful accomplishments. Giving back can become part of everyone's job description, and with that opportunity and responsibility incredible things can happen. Every company can and should help to repair the world. It is every bit as good for the company as it is for the world we live in. And it's the best way to build a corporate purpose and a corporate legacy. It extends you—and lives on.

HOW TO INCORPORATE GIVING BACK INTO WORK

- **Stick with what you believe in.** When we first introduced the Liquidnet for Good idea, our board at that time was not completely supportive with our approach. They argued that philanthropy was a personal choice, not a corporate mission. They said we were a growing business, and didn't have time for this. Even our employees were mixed about it at first. "That's going to come out of my bonus," some of them complained. I was adamant and knew it was the right thing to do. It would be good for the world, our corporate soul and a great way to get the right people in the door.

- **Provide employees and their families with a way to make the world a better place and unite them through a common goal and purpose.** Hundreds of Liquidnet employees, family members, and friends, through volunteer work, have contributed their time, resources, and passion to turn the idea for the ASYV into a reality. They've helped from assisting with the initial strategic plans to serving on organizing committees to engaging in skill based volunteer trips. More than 1,000 young people have called ASYV home in its first eight years. We also launched a global fundraising platform called Race for Rwanda so that everyone, everywhere could participate. Since 2007, more than 100 Liquidnet family members have competed in different competitions around the world—from the NYC Triathlon to Spartan high-endurance races in Sydney to color runs, 5-day races across the world's largest deserts, and many more—raising more than half a million dollars for the village.

- **Leverage your strengths.** Since 2001, we've created greater efficiency within the capital markets through the use of technology. What we have found is that we can leverage what we've learned in the financial markets to make other markets more efficient—specifically, the nonprofit market, which we call Markets for Good, another major project of Liquidnet for Good. There is very little data about how these nonprofits perform compared to one another, how effective their outcomes are, or anything regarding their returns on their investments. We believe that by employing the best aspects of market dynamics, feedback loops, structured data and information, and common comparative metrics, we can help maximize the impact of philanthropic funding. By providing more transparency of information and by making it more simple and organized, we can massively increase the flow of dollars, direct those dollars to those organizations that are most efficiently fulfilling their mission statement, and, ultimately, solve many more problems.

- **Champion causes that are important to your employees.** We have funded a wide range of programs from our "Double Down" matching gift program, which allows employees to maximize their support for the causes most important to them. We not only match their personal donations but the time they invest in supporting organizations important to them. We also recently introduced "Double Down I Earth" to incentivize and encourage employees to make environmental sustainability a part of daily lives by reimbursing employees for up to 50 percent of the costs of green products and services, from energy-efficient appliances to home weatherizing to bike share programs. Our local impact grants enable employees to nominate charitable organizations that work in the local community. So far, hundreds of thousands of dollars in grants have gone to dozens of worthy groups around the globe.

It's Not a Zero-Sum Game

Too often, too many see business as a zero sum game. That in order for me to win somebody has to lose. But that's a false notion—and a dangerous one.

If there is one overall lesson I've learned in my career, it's that you can build a great company, make a lot of money, do it honestly, and do good work at the same time.

I started out on Wall Street, which has long been defined by a culture that I define as how fast I can take money out of your pocket and put it in mine. It is for the most part an "eat what you kill" model. Employees get some percentage of the revenue that they generate, which means that everybody is his or her own profit center within their respective firms.

By not following that model—by looking at the industry through a different lens, by looking past business as usual and fixing the root of some very large problems that most people considered the cost of doing business, making business a team sport, having some fun while you are doing it, you can make a difference. You will improve some part of this world, you will positively impact the lives of your employees and your customers, and I hope that you will spend time and energy giving your employees an opportunity to make this world a better place. After all, work is where you spend much of your life. Life is short, and you only have one to live. You should do everything you can to make it count.

• • •

The Liquidnet Interview:
Cultural Fit Questions

*T**he following questions have been created to assist us in determining whether candidates are a Liquidnet culture fit, and whether they will be successful here. We assign specific questions at the interview team pre-huddle.*

The Liquidnet Experience

We Are Laser-Focused and Know When to Say "No"
- Tell me about a time when you had clear deliverables and a supervisor or head of another department asked for your assistance/for you to take something else on. How did you handle it?
- It is goal-setting time. You and your boss have set some exciting goals for you and your team. You then realize, given the existing workload and bandwidth, that these are more "nice to have" than must-haves. How do you handle this?

Accountability and Empowerment Are in Harmony
- Tell me about a time when you worked on a team project and it was unclear who was in charge. What did you do?
- What would you do if you saw another employee acting out at a networking event and it clearly was not in the best interest of the company?

Honesty
- Think about a time when you were asked to provide specific information to a client/partner/other external party, but you

knew that the information would not be positive. What did you do?

- Tell me about a time when you maintained high ethical standards despite pressure to do otherwise.
- Describe a situation where you observed someone being dishonest. How did you respond?

Innovation/Problem Solving

- Give me an example where you developed an unusual solution to a problem. What inspired you to come up with that?

Continuous Learner/Development

- What do you do to stay current in your field and at work in general?
- Tell me about a time when you were asked to change the way you do something.

Global Mind-Set

- Describe a time when you sought input from your coworkers globally, before making an important decision.
- Tell me about a time when you neglected to solicit input from your global business partners. What was the result? How did you address it?
- What are some of the challenges of running a global team? How do you handle them?

Other

Political

- Describe the corporate culture of your last two to three employers. What worked? What didn't?
- Tell me of a time you observed office politics:
  - What did it look like?
  - What impact did it have on the organization or the person?
  - What did you do; what action(s) did you take?
- Tell me about a time when you made a mistake and someone was blamed for your error. How did you handle it?
- How would you respond if your manager told you that you could not speak directly to their manager or to the CEO without coming to her/him first?

Know It All

- Tell me about a time when you learned something significant from a junior person.
- Imagine that you had to hire your team completely from scratch. What kind of team would you create? What skills, knowledge, expertise, and viewpoints would you seek? How would these differ from what you bring to the table?
- Tell me a time when you thought you knew better and discovered that you didn't.
- What was the biggest mistake you ever made?

Listening

- Rate your listening skills on scale of 1 to 10 (10 being the best).
- Describe what makes you a good listener.
- Have you ever received feedback that you need to work on your listening skills? If so, what did you do about it?
- Tell me about a time when you felt that you weren't being heard. What made you believe that the other party wasn't listening, and how does that impact the way that you listen to others?
- Tell me about a time when your supervisor or someone above you gave you an assignment, but his/her instructions and expectations weren't clear. How did you handle this?
- Tell me about a time when you were in a meeting and passionately disagreed with someone's opinion. How do you convey your point of view?

Collaboration

- How would you define a collaborative environment?
  - What does it look like?
  - Give me an example when you chose to collaborate with others when you could have done it alone.
  - Tell me about a time when you pulled back on your own goals for the sake of the team. Why did you do this, and what was the outcome?
  - Research tells us that as an organization matures, the culture tends to become less collaborative. How do you think an organization can prevent this from happening?
  - Tell me about a time when you chose *not* to collaborate. Why was this? What was the result?

Afterword: You Can Invent the Future

When I first decided to write this book in 2013, life was normal. Liquidnet was coming out of the mess ignited by the financial crisis, and I was confident the company would survive. All the battles won and lost came with lessons learned, tactics improved, and stories to share. Anne, my partner and soul mate, was radiantly alive and we were dreaming again about our future.

It turned out that Liquidnet was far from out of the woods and I could never in my worst nightmare dream of what was yet to come. After Anne's accident, I had nothing left. Work was incredibly tough, but home was worse—there was no respite. There was no escape, and then there were the projects that Anne had been working on, especially the Agahozo-Shalom Youth Village that I had to make sure continued to thrive through what would be a very difficult transition.

In the weeks following the accident I knew I had to go to the Village in Rwanda. The kids living in the Village were worried that without Anne, whom they called "mother" or "grandmother," the Village would close and they would again suffer the loss of their home and their new family. The Village that began as just a thought and became a reality through Anne's sheer will and perseverance absolutely had to continue. The kids needed to see me and hear me tell them that I would make sure the village would always go on. When I arrived and spoke at the most beautiful memorial service I had ever experienced, I told them that as their father I wanted to hug each and every one living there. Before I finished speaking, they started lining up—500 kids and 300 house mothers, cooks, gardeners, volunteers, and all the other people who worked there. It was amazing, and I needed their hugs as much as they needed mine.

The name of the village, Agahozo-Shalom, is a combination of a Kinyarwanda word and a Hebrew word that means "a place where tears are dried" and "peace." Anne knew it was the perfect name from the moment my daughter Jenna came up with it, but I never once imagined that it would be a place where *my* tears would be dried. That's what happened. In seeing the miracle that Anne created in every one of the kids' faces, I couldn't help but feel so proud.

Everyone deals with grief differently. I turned my attention to work and staying incredibly busy from that point on. It was too hard to go home, so I searched for ways to keep myself occupied. As if fixing Liquidnet wasn't enough of a challenge, I started three new businesses: a biotech investment fund, which raised $40 million to invest in promising cures for monogenetic diseases; a pharmaceutical company I started with my father that looks for bioactive compounds in Israeli desert plants; and, to complete Anne's vision of creating businesses to help the village become self-sustaining, a solar company in Africa that installs solar panels on people's huts to provide electricity to their homes for the first time.

Based in Rwanda, but serving all of Africa, it will employ graduates of the ASYV to install and maintain the panels and run the call center. The Village will also get a portion of the company revenue. The solar business will be the start to making the AYSV sustainable and enable it, hopefully, to outlive us all.

Two years after Anne's accident, working constantly, boarding a plane every other day and out to dinners every night, time and fatigue caught up with me and I realized I was tired of being sad all the time and I had to deal with the pain. I began therapy and slowly over time, I am starting to find ways to enjoy life again.

Liquidnet celebrated its 15-year anniversary and everything we have done to turn the company around continues to pay off. The big banks continue to retrench, and I have never been more optimistic about our prospects of taking market share and expanding into new businesses. The AYSV continues to thrive and the kids continue to excel at everything they do from scoring at the very top of the country in their matriculation exams, to winning national sports and debate tournaments. I'm thrilled that one of the first graduates of the village interned at Liquidnet this summer.

I'm traveling less, but not slowing down. I am extremely excited about the opportunities that we have created for ourselves, and I'm eager to start fixing some of the huge problems that still plague our industry. The prospects for positive destruction never end, and in this I've found a renewed purpose.

● ● ●

One month before her accident, Anne told a friend that if she died that day she would have lived a very full life. I believe that those who have the opportunity to live a full life have the obligation to do so—that can include working to invent a new future in a company or industry to helping to make the world a better place.

Positive destruction is just what it means. It is breaking things down to put them back together better. It improves productivity, jobs, companies, industries, economies, and the lives of all the people who benefit from those improvements.

What's happening in your company, in your industry, in your life? Pick something you're excited about and define a very large problem, then figure out the one, two, or three things that, if you really solved for, would give you an unfair competitive advantage and your prospects would be stupid not to buy from you.

Think about ways you can incorporate philanthropy, about ways you want to give back. We all own the obligation to repair the world, and if every person and every company took on some of that responsibility, the world would indeed be a better place. I can tell you from experience that dedicating yourself to something bigger than money, more important than power or prestige, is what will sustain you and give you purpose when times are tough. Success and happiness can be mercurial, but finding meaning and doing good for others is a gift that keeps on giving and what will keep you going.

Use the tools in this book to help you detail your tactics, design your plan, stack the deck in your favor—and win. You can benefit from knowing that most people don't spend the time and energy to figure out their company's unfair competitive advantage and unique selling proposition. Simply being better prepared than your competition helps stack the deck in your favor.

I'm now living in a new and altered world I would never have designed, but we all live in a world that alters itself every day and makes it hard for us to keep up. We must adapt to these sometimes unbelievably difficult realities. The pace of change only seems to increase, and that means that more companies, business models, and industries will be disrupted faster.

I started and completed this book for those of you who are excited by the opportunity to make a difference, to change a company or industry and make it better. I believe that every bit of positive destruction makes the world a little better. Good luck following your passion to find your problem, create your opportunity, and invent a better future.

Index